PAPER AND TALK

Edited by Nicholas Thieberger

A manual for reconstituting materials in Australian
Indigenous languages from historical sources

PAPER
AND TALK

ABORIGINAL
STUDIES
PRESS

First published in 1995 by

Aboriginal Studies Press for the Australian Institute of Aboriginal and Torres Strait Islander Studies
GPO Box 553
Canberra ACT 2601

Reprinted 2005, 2026

The views expressed in this publication are those of the author and not necessarily those of the Australian Institute of Aboriginal and Torres Strait Islander Studies.

National Library of Australia
Cataloguing-in-Publication data:

Paper and talk: a manual for reconstituting materials in Australian indigenous languages from historical sources.
    Bibliography.
    ISBN 0 85575 273 4.

    1. Australian languages. 2. Extinct languages. 3. Reconstruction (Linguistics) — Methodology. I. Thieberger, Nicholas.

499.15

Lament for a dialect
Mary Duroux

Dyirringan is lost to the tribes of
    the Yuin
I am filled with remorse
    and I weep at the ruin
Of beautiful words
    that were softly spoken
Now lay in the past
    all shattered and broken
We forgot it somehow
    when English began
The sweet-sounding dialect
    of Dyirringan
If we're to be civilised
    whom can we blame
To have lost you
    my language
    is my greatest shame

Bill Reid passed away in early November 1993. He was very positive about recording his language, Gamilaraay, and he was an enthusiastic participant in the Paper and Talk workshop. Here is an edited version of his welcome speech.

Welcome

 am very happy to have been invited to this workshop, and I'm grateful to those who worked towards getting me down here, because I'm an old-age pensioner, and I suppose my resources are very limited. I'm grateful to the Institute for being able to get me here.

I was asked at a meeting in Bourke to make a welcome speech at a particular celebration, and to give it some sort of prestige they wanted me to say welcome to the people in my language. They wanted it in the Wangkumara language, but I'm Gamilaraay, I'm not Wangkumara. So I composed a little speech in Gamilaraay. On that particular day I wanted them to forget, forget the bad things and to remember that we have many good things going for us. And so I had to go on then in English and explain the good things, legal aid, medical service and all those types of things that we had going for us. But I was pleased to be able to give it some quality, some Aboriginal quality, put something into the meeting that we had that day.

And so we have in front of us a great lot of work to do, a large amount of good work, and I'm glad the linguists are here today, they can pick those bits and pieces and maybe throw me out of the meeting.

Anyways, I'm sure that we're going to get a whole lot out of this workshop, and I'm looking forward to what we will get, for the input of all of the people. I'm grateful to Janet Mathews who used to come out and I used a lot of her grandfather's stuff to get the words that I know now. And I just found another excellent book, discovered by accident, it was mixed up in my stuff, and it was the Bible stories of Ridley. There's words there I didn't know about. The spelling of those people is atrocious! One spells a word one way, another spells it another way, it's just a big mix up. I'm hoping that we can standardise our language, the halfway sounds that we've got, the p and the b, the t and d, the j and y, the k instead of the g and all of this muck up with the English alphabet, and we've got to try and work out some system of standardising the spelling even if we've got to put the p and the b together. Each of these with a double meaning, spell them the same way so that they know what they're on about.

I hope that we can get a lot out of this workshop.

Bill Reid
May 1993

T his book is the result of a workshop held at AIATSIS (Australian Institute of Aboriginal and Torres Strait Islander Studies) in March 1993. It aims to give information to language workers about taking texts and wordlists from historical sources and making them useful in language programs and literature today. What we present in this book is a quick guide to what are really very complicated issues. If you want to find out more, look at Crowley's introduction to historical linguistics (Crowley 1992).

Introduction

Finding out about languages that are no longer spoken, or are still spoken by only a few people, can be a long and difficult project. It needs a certain amount of detective work to go through old sources and to make them useful to language projects today. If you are lucky you may also have material recorded by trained linguists, and audio tapes to help decipher the relation between written forms and the sounds they are meant to represent. Making sense of the information you find can also take a great deal of work. Some recording of Australian indigenous languages in the early days was quite good, but much of it was done by people who were not able to hear the sounds of Australian languages, nor were they expecting to find complicated grammars, or a rich understanding of the natural environment.

The late Bill Reid worked to recover his language from his own memory and from written sources. His opening address cautions about the spelling used in old sources, and advises that linguists can be quite useful.

Jeanie Bell, although not at the workshop, has written of her experience in putting together a dictionary of her grandmother's language from historical material including more recent material recorded by a trained linguist (Chapter 1).

Finding out which language was spoken in a particular place may also be difficult. While there are strong links between Australian languages and the country of their speakers, these links can also change over time. Nicholas Thieberger (Chapter 2) looks at these issues and suggests books to look at for more details on language names and locations.

Jaki Troy discusses some of the problems in reading handwriting that is difficult to read (Chapter 4). The original sources may be hard to find, located in a collection in a capital city, or elsewhere in the world. Geraldine Triffitt (Chapter 3) suggests where to look for historical material.

How do you figure out how to pronounce the words written in historical sources? Peter Austin and Terry Crowley (Chapter 5) outline a method for taking words spelled in a number of ways from a number of sources and figuring out what they could or should sound like. They show that comparison with neighbouring languages can help, and also discuss the types of typographical errors that can be spotted with a little knowledge of the type of language you are working with. Charts of different spelling systems in use in parts of Australia show what type of sounds to expect (Chapter 6). Nicholas Thieberger also compares the way sounds are made in a few languages and in English.

There is more to a language than words, so we need to understand the grammar and how words are used in building sentences. Jane Simpson (Chapter 7) describes the most common type of grammatical patterns found in Australian languages and the way in which old sources can hold more information about grammar than may be thought at first glance.

Once you have made sense of the information, what can you do with it? Rob Amery (Chapter 8) emphasises the importance of getting language back into use in various ways, including greetings, songs and other everyday activities.

Computers are a useful tool in reworking historical materials. Nicholas Thieberger (Chapter 9) provides an example of the transformation of a handwritten manuscript into a useful set of electronic data.

Many historical sources have been reworked and are now available in a more accessible format. A list of some wordlists and dictionaries based on historical sources is included as Appendix 2.

A list of participants at the workshop can be found in Appendix 1. Some of the exercises and activities at the workshop are included in this book. One that is not is the transcription of tapes which many of the participants found very useful. The sound archive at AIATSIS supplied a short example of taped material from relevant languages and the workshop split into groups to work on transcribing some of the tape. A similar exercise can be provided for you to work with your own language, if you give the sound archive at AIATSIS enough notice to prepare a sample tape. ■

Jeanie Bell

Working on a dictionary for Murri languages

Working on a dictionary for Murri languages

ver since I have been involved in working with Murri languages, I have wondered whether there would be an opportunity for me to work with my own languages from south-east Queensland. Initially I believed that because our languages were no longer spoken there would be little chance for this to happen, even though at that time I had no idea of what material was available in the archives, museums, historical societies and libraries, and indeed I didn't even know how many people from these language groups had some knowledge of the languages.

So when I went to work in the Northern Territory on the living languages of Central Australia, I became aware of how important it was to our identity as indigenous people to have that connection to our language and our culture. Also, in order for us to function as healthy people this connection and understanding had to be there. For some groups of Aboriginal people in this country these links have never been broken due to their geographical isolation, their late exposure to the more ruthless sides of colonisation, and even a late introduction to the so-called benefits of the English language, both oracy and literacy. These groups of people have been fortunate enough to be able to maintain the strength of their language and culture, sometimes in the face of quite extraordinary circumstances, particularly the impact of English and all that means.

Even in some parts of the east coast, this situation has been quite different from one group to the other, depending on the development factors in that region, and the type of missionaries or government supervisors they were exposed to during the decades of missionisation and christianisation, and then, of course, of integration and assimilation. However, in south-east Queensland, the colonisation, decimation, dislocation, alienation and dispossession process was very fast and brutal. Many of our languages were killed off very quickly with many of our people. Our old people were rounded up and put on reserves, and brainwashed and brutalised until they quite often believed themselves that they were lesser human beings than the whites who ruled their lives. The only way they could ever be considered acceptable, but never equal, was if they forgot their traditional culture, practices, beliefs and languages and copied the ways that were being forced upon them. During all of this, they were constantly reminded that they could never be as good as the white models they were exposed to (which weren't all that great anyway), but would always be regarded in an inferior way.

When I finally got back home and started working on my own languages, I had worked through some of these issues and developed a better understanding of it all, not only from our experience in this part of the country, but in the fuller perspective of what had happened in other parts of the country as well. So when I got my first small grant to work on compiling the dictionary, I think I was coming at it from a different angle to what I might have done even five years before that, and I think that was an important part of the process.

I had to do a bit of work in collecting copies of as much of the historical information as I could, but there was a lot of local knowledge by this stage of what was available and what was considered a useful source and what wasn't, so I just went about the business of collecting all this material, and started to study it. Of course, most importantly, I had to make contact with the Elders from our group, and any remaining speakers who I could identify and who were accessible. Unfortunately, the numbers of people were very small, and even in terms of Elders there are only a few of them left, and they are fairly spread out, so this meant that I couldn't always have regular contact with them. Also, because they are very old and such a valuable resource in our community, there is quite a lot of demand on their time and knowledge, and we have to be very conscious of this in making any added demands on them.

I had some funds to work on the dictionary full-time for about three months, and most of this time was spent doing the research and keying the information into the computer. There were a lot of other similar projects happening around different parts of Australia at this time, so it was a good time and environment in which to be doing this work. Also, it was a time when more and more Murries were getting involved in this kind of work, and even though there had been a belief that it was essential that formally trained linguists be the main people involved in this work, Murries were standing up at different meetings which were organised to discuss language issues and saying that they were taking more control over these types of activities, and now wanted to have more say in the direction which these projects would take.

So I guess I was in a fairly privileged position of having done linguistics study at university, been out to work in Central Australia with some living languages, and now returned to my own country where cultural and linguistic revival was becoming a real factor in our lives.

One of the issues which kept coming up was the question of access to this material, particularly for other Murries from the same language group, but also for Murries living in the area where these languages were spoken, or non-Murries interested in the language for various reasons. People were anxious to get it once they knew it was in the pipeline, and of course even now there are many requests for copies of this material. Of course we then had to deal with issues of copyright and ownership, and when I had been given the first small dictionary grant from AIATSIS in Canberra, I had to negotiate with them about copyright, and the only terms on which I would accept the grant were if they would agree to let the copyright of the material remain with the Gubbi Gubbi and Butchulla people. So when the dictionary is finally printed the copyright of this material will belong to the present Gubbi Gubbi and Butchulla people who are the traditional owners of their tribal lands, and of the cultural and linguistic heritage which goes with the responsibility of custodianship of land and lore. They will be the people who decide who has access to the material and how this information and knowledge is used. First and foremost, we must always respect the words of the Elders in this regard, and then make sure that we use this knowledge with the integrity and respect that it is due.

Finally having access to this information after so long a period of denial and alienation from our language will play a major role in strengthening our identity and our traditional links to this land and our ancestors. We are not idealistic about our languages becoming fully spoken languages again, or that they might replace the role of English for us, but they certainly will fill an enormous vacuum in our lives, which has been forced upon us for too long. We want people to understand what this means to us, but we also want people to respect our right to lay claim to our connections to this land together with all the traditional rights and responsibilities which this brings.

Times have changed dramatically in the past twenty years, and with these changes, there have developed other fears and concerns by the non-Aboriginal people of this country, and until they can come to terms with their own place in this country and the role that their ancestors may have played in steering this country to its present day state — that is, owning their own history (and not necessarily having to feel guilty) — then we will never get any closer to understanding and accepting each other as equal players in the future of this land.

For while they and their peers and families continue to consider us as second-class citizens, the poor relations dependent on their goodwill and continued welfare handouts, and refuse to see us in any other role, there will always be resentment from our camp because we know more than anything that there is a basic lack of respect for who we are and where we have come from and where we are going to. ■

Nicholas Thieberger

What is your language?

What is your language?

Trying to find out what language your grandparents or great-grandparents spoke can be difficult. What they called their language may be different from what other people called it, or what the written records call it. Or they may never have told you what language they spoke.

There are usually a few names for a language or a group of people who speak a language. This should not be too surprising — think of *Australians*, who speak *English*, but might also be *Western Australians*, or *sandgropers*, or *Nyungars*. They could also be *wajalas* or *balanda* (terms used by Aboriginal people to refer to Europeans). You can see that there are at least seven terms which could be used to name these people, and the name of their language can sometimes be (or get confused with) the name of the group. If you also consider that outsiders have names for these people, then you also have such names as *Australiens, Australiani* or *Orang Australi*. Naming language groups can be difficult, but finding out what language was a person's main language may not be easy either. Because many Aboriginal people are multilingual, they could also identify themselves with a number of languages. If you know what language a relative spoke, it could also be the language you are after. If you need help with finding relations you could look at the Aboriginal Studies Press book, *Lookin for Your Mob* (Smith and Halstead 1990).

If you know what place your language belongs to, you can then go to a map to find out which group's country it is. The map people

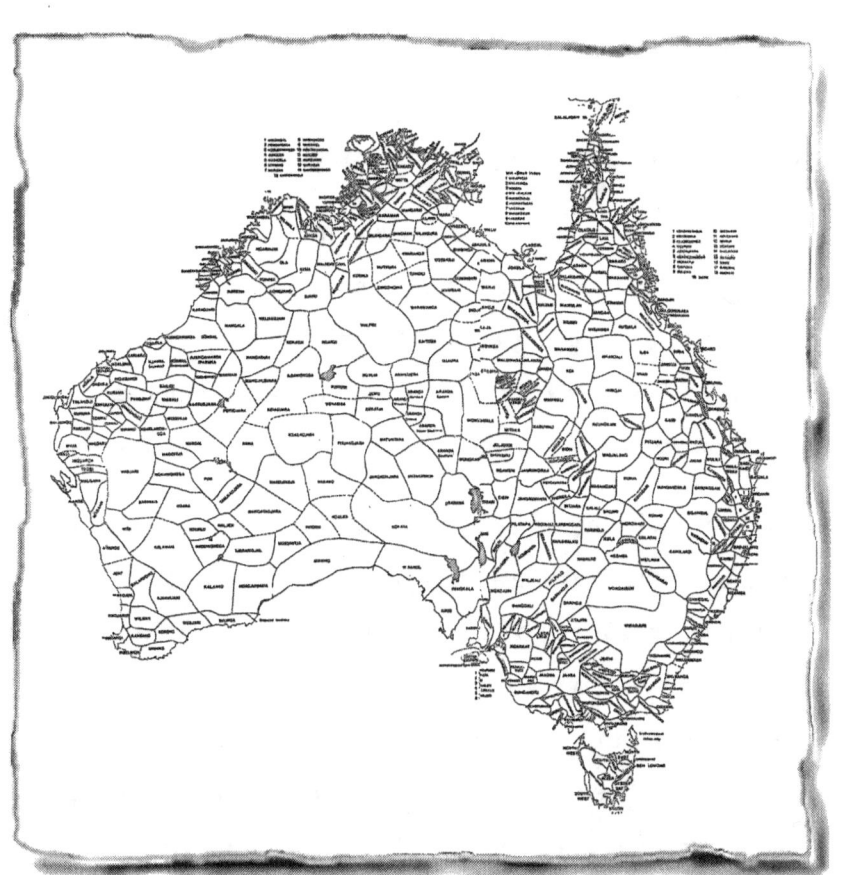

usually refer to is Tindale (1974); it is the big map (above) with the whole country divided up with boundaries clearly defined between the named groups. Given that there could be lots of different names for one group of people, Tindale's map on its own is not always going to provide the answer you want. The books accompanying the map give more detail and some alternative names for the groups on the map. It is doubtful whether the boundaries and territories he shows on the map should ever have been taken to be permanent and unchangeable things. You should also bear in mind that Tindale travelled around the country collecting the information for his map, and that what he recorded depended on who he talked to, and how much he understood local languages (which is generally very little).

There are other maps around, some better than others, but not all of them aim to show the same thing. Some of them try to show traditional territories from before the European invasion. Others try to show what groups are still speaking languages today, or are still associated with certain parts of the country.

If you are lucky there may be more detailed work available for the area you are looking at. If there are good records of the language, like a grammar or collection of texts, then these will provide the best source of information for you. You should also get in touch with those researchers who have worked in your area, and also see if there are any language centres around that could help (see Appendix 3 for a list of these). ■

Helpful books

General works which list information about Australian languages are: Capell (1963); Oates (1975); O'Grady, Voegelin and Voegelin (1966); Tindale (1974); Wurm (1972).

In some parts of the country there are handbooks available. For the Northern Territory see Black (1983), and Menning and Nash (1981); a handbook of Top End languages is also in preparation. For Western Australia see McGregor (1988) and Thieberger (1993).

**Geraldine
Triffitt**

What is written on your language?

How do you obtain access to it?

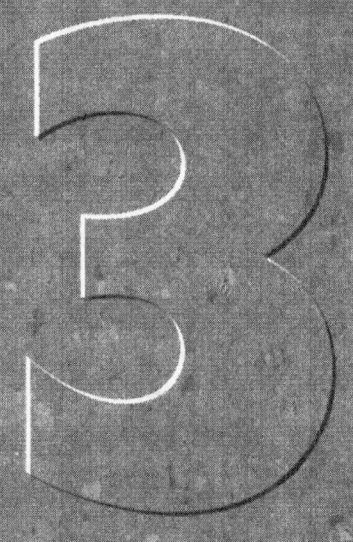

What is written on your language?

In this chapter I will describe some of the wordlists, sentences and texts that explorers, settlers, missionaries, and government officials recorded from Aboriginal people in the early days of European contact. Then I will outline the work undertaken this century, by visiting scholars, students and staff of university linguistics departments, and lately by Aboriginal linguistic workers at language centres. Finally, I will give a brief description of where these materials are located and how you may obtain access, beginning with the library of the Australian Institute of Aboriginal and Torres Strait Islander Studies.

Early language records

New South Wales

Following the material collected by David Collins, William Dawes, the Astronomer, and other officers involved in the early settlement in Australia, interest in learning the local languages, recording words and analysing grammar was mainly conducted by missionaries. Threlkeld in the Lake Macquarie area and Günther in Wellington Valley recorded Awabakal and Wiradjuri respectively. Their material was used by Horatio Hale, Linguist with the United States Exploring Expedition in 1838–1842.

Victoria

Apart from some poor wordlists recorded by George Augustus Robinson in the 1840s and an English–Aboriginal vocabulary of the Melbourne language by Daniel Bunce in 1851, most of the recordings of Victorian languages were published by Brough Smyth in 1878, including Green's vocabulary of the Yarra tribe and Thomas' Woiwurrung material. James Dawson wrote an account of three local tribes of the Western District, including wordlists, in 1881.

Tasmania

Despite visits by English explorers, and subsequent British settlement, the earliest ethnographic and linguistic information recorded was by French expeditions of Baudin and D'Entrecasteaux. In the period 1823–1834, George Augustus Robinson recorded vocabulary in his journals, and during their visit to the colonies in 1832 and 1838, Backhouse and Walker recorded vocabulary and songs on Flinders Island. Milligan compiled a vocabulary published in 1857 as a parliamentary paper and reprinted by Brough Smyth and others. Unfortunately only a few sentences and songs were recorded and no attempt was made to analyse the grammar.

Western Australia

Captain George Grey recognised similarities in sound and structure among different languages and suggested that the languages belonged to a language family. Bishop Salvado (at New Norcia), Francis Armstrong, George Fletcher Moore and R.M. Lyon recorded languages of the south-west.

Queensland

The earliest recorded material from a language in Queensland was of Guugu Yimithirr of which Sir Joseph Banks recorded 180 words (including 'kangaroo'). In 1843, 15 words of the Hinchinbrook dialect of Warrgamay were collected during the voyage of the HMS *Fly*, and another 200 words were collected in 1884 by Houzé and Jacques. Another Warrgamay dialect was described by the Norwegian zoologist, Lumholtz, in 1889 as having a small vocabulary and lack of abstract expressions, and his misconceptions affected attitudes to Australian languages for many years.

Northern Territory

During the short-lived settlement at Raffles Bay, Cobourg Peninsula, the commandant, Captain Collet Barker, attempted to learn the language of the people there. His diary, held at the Mitchell Library, Sydney, records his attempts. Earl, a competent linguist, was among the first settlers at Port Essington. He noticed the influence of Macassan words in the local languages. In 1846, the shipwrecked Father Angelo Confalonieri worked as a missionary at Port Essington and recorded some of the Iwaidja language. A vocabulary of the Woolner District of the Adelaide River, compiled by J.W.O. Bennett, was published by Taplin in 1879.

South Australia

Shortly after the establishment of the South Australian colony in 1836, Lutheran missionaries Teichelmann and Schürmann worked among the Kaurna people in Adelaide and learned and recorded their language. Another German missionary, Meyer, recorded the language of Encounter Bay (Ngarrindjeri) in 1843, a language studied by George Taplin, founder of the Aborigines' Friends Association mission at Point McLeay.

n the latter part of the nineteenth century, interest in Aboriginal languages and particularly in the differences between them was renewed. Projects to collect language lists from government officials, or settlers in particular areas, culminated in the publication of the vocabularies in Curr's *The Australian Race*, covering the whole continent. Howitt received some language lists from his correspondents who sent him details about Aboriginal social organisation. Ridley, a missionary, analysed the languages of Northern New South Wales, and R.H. Mathews collected ethnological information, wordlists and grammatical information while he worked as a surveyor in various parts of Australia. The journal *Science of Man*, published by the Anthropological Society of Australasia, provided a forum for local settlers, government officials and other interested people to send in snippets of local language, and particularly placenames. The visiting linguist, Sydney Ray, collected Aboriginal vocabularies from north-west Australia and, whilst with the Cambridge Anthropological Expedition, recorded the languages of Torres Strait.

Later works

Nineteenth century governments had passed legislation to 'protect' the original inhabitants, and many of the Protectors of Aborigines, notably W.E. Roth and Archibald Meston of Queensland, had recorded features of the languages.

Interest then languished until the 1950s except for some isolated linguistic activity by missionaries like Nekes and Worms in the Kimberleys, and by notable individuals, Daisy Bates for example, and a few academics. Baldwin Spencer and Gerhardt Laves recorded vocabulary from various regions during their sojourn in Australia in the 1920s. Anthropologists Stanner, Tindale, Elkin and their students, and linguists Arthur Capell, T.G.H. Strehlow and Stephen Wurm were ahead of their time in recording social organisation, ceremony and language in various parts of Australia. Geoffrey O'Grady recorded information from languages all over the country. The Summer Institute of Linguistics (an organisation devoted to Bible translation) held its first courses in Melbourne in 1951.

In 1958–60 the eminent American linguist, Ken Hale, visited Australia and collected a large amount of vernacular language material spoken in the Northern Territory, Queensland, northern Western Australia and particularly central Australia. From the texts and elicited sentences and vocabulary, he analysed grammar and sentence structure and came to understand the worldview of the people he learned from.

Hale's visit was the trigger for the rebirth of academic interest in Australian languages. Linguistics had been taught within the Department of Anthropology, University of Sydney, since 1926. When William Hoddinott took up the Chair of English at the University of New England, he became interested in the languages of northern New South Wales, the Daly River region of the Northern Territory and the Kununurra area of the Kimberleys.

In 1965, Monash University founded the first independent department of linguistics, followed by the Australian National University's Faculty of Arts department in 1970 and Newcastle and Sydney in 1975. Other linguistic stimulus came from the establishment by Act of Parliament in 1964 of the Australian Institute of Aboriginal Studies, and of the publishing medium, Pacific Linguistics, in 1966 (formerly the Linguistic Circle of Canberra).

With the increase of post-graduate students and other researchers recording and analysing languages, the archives of tape recordings and fieldnotes held at the Institute grew rapidly. The Institute library has acquired as much published material on Aboriginal topics as possible using Greenway's *Bibliography of the Australian Aborigines and the Native Peoples of Torres Strait to 1959* (Sydney: Angus and Robertson, 1963) as a first guide.

How do you obtain access to materials?

 aving briefly discussed the sources of linguistic material recorded before 1960, how do you obtain access to it?

Many of the wordlists described above have been published. The early vocabularies collected by scholars accompanying explorers are usually published in the diary of the voyage or expedition or in accounts of first settlers. For instance, there is a Sydney vocabulary at the end of David Collins' *An Account of the English Colony in New South Wales.* Horatio Hale wrote volume five of the *Reports of the United States Exploring Expedition under the Command of Charles Wilkes* (Philadelphia: 1846).

Resources at AIATSIS Library

Published works like the above are in the library at the Australian Institute of Aboriginal and Torres Strait Islander Studies (AIATSIS). The Institute has a comprehensive catalogue, including material which is not held there. The information is held on the Institute's computer, and searches for references on particular languages are undertaken from the catalogue on request. There is a charge for this service.

Other locations of books, serials and manuscript collections are given on the Australian Bibliographical Network which links libraries throughout Australia. This is usually accessible from a local public library which can arrange interlibrary loans of books or photocopies of articles from magazines and journals.

However, some vocabularies, grammar notes and even stories are not published but remain in manuscript form. AIATSIS has a large collection of unpublished material. As a condition of its research grants, the Institute stipulates that copies of fieldnotes and recordings of linguistic work must be deposited in its library. Copies of these works must also be returned to the communities which have provided the information. With increasing academic linguistic research, large collections of manuscripts and tape recordings, and the resulting theses, have been added to the Institute's collections.

Some of the results of linguistic fieldwork undertaken before the establishment of the Institute are also in the library. Vocabulary lists collected by the surveyor R.H. Mathews and placenames correspondence sent to F.D. McCarthy while he was at the Australian Museum are stored in the library.

The originals and copies of Gerhardt Laves' vocabularies, sentences and texts including languages of New South Wales are fully indexed. They were sent from the United States where they were stored in an attic for many years. Unfortunately, the storage was inadequate and water obliterated much of the writing on the cards. This is an example of the need for proper storage and preservation of records.

Among the large Stanner collection of fieldnotes, papers and publications are some linguistic notes from the Daly River area.

Some of William Hoddinott's collection of stories, songs, vocabulary and texts from the New England and north coast areas of New South Wales have accompanying tapes.

Copies of the fieldnotes from Ken Hale's visits to Australia have been deposited in the Institute. His Warlpiri notes form the basis of the Warlpiri dictionary, produced at the Institute for Aboriginal Development in Alice Springs.

Unpublished material and tapes deposited at the Institute remain under the control of the depositor, who can request restrictions on access or copying of material. In some cases this may be because secret language is used, or it may be that the material is in a preliminary form, or that it will be published later.

Other sources

Not all of the historic linguistic material is at AIATSIS. Although other libraries may have the originals, in many cases AIATSIS has copies of the manuscripts. This means that the material may be seen at AIATSIS but permission to copy material remains with the holding institution. For example, the South Australian Museum holds some of the records of the early missionaries, Schürmann and Reuther, as well as the papers of the anthropologist Norman Tindale who collected more than 100 vocabularies during his visit with the Harvard Australian Expedition in 1938–39, and more vocabularies from the Gulf of Carpentaria region in 1960 and 1963.

In Melbourne, the La Trobe Library holds the correspondence of Brough Smyth, and the papers of Howitt which include kinship terms among his notes on social organisation, and the papers of Baldwin Spencer, who recorded grammatical expressions from some of the Top End Northern Territory languages.

The Elkin papers are at the University of Sydney Archives. They include linguistic notes collected in the Kimberley region of Western Australia. The large body of linguistic material of Australia and the Pacific amassed by Arthur Capell is located temporarily with his literary executor but will eventually come to AIATSIS in Canberra.

The Mitchell Library, as the repository of material written in or about New South Wales, has the original manuscript vocabularies collected by George Augustus Robinson in his wanderings around Tasmania and south-eastern Victoria and New South Wales. Another manuscript located there is one of the few records of Guring-gai, the language spoken North of Port Jackson, which the missionary Threlkeld recorded.

In Brisbane, the Oxley Library collects information about Queensland. It has the reports of the Protectors, including Roth and Meston who recorded many wordlists. Thanks to the efforts of D.D. Bannister, a language enthusiast, copies of these lists and compilations of languages around Brisbane are in the AIATSIS library.

The National Library of Australia, in Canberra, has large holdings of personal manuscripts including the notebooks and vocabularies collected by Daisy Bates on her travels in Western Australia.

Some wordlists have come from further afield. The Confalonieri manuscripts belong to the Propaganda Fide Archive, Rome. The Dawes manuscripts, which have the most complete records of the grammar and vocabulary of the Sydney language, are located at the Library of the School of Oriental and Asian Studies, London, but copies have been deposited in AIATSIS library.

Recognition of the need to bring together all available material in languages under threat of extinction motivated the series *Handbook of Australian Languages*, edited by R.M.W. Dixon and Barry Blake. For each language included there is a description of past records and research, a sketch grammar and comprehensive wordlist. Community-based language centres are now collecting material in the languages of their areas to publish stories, grammars and wordlists for use in schools.

It should be noted that researchers may have to meet the specific requirements of the holding organisation in other States or Territories before material becomes available. This may include applying for a reader's ticket giving the reasons for wanting the ticket together with a statement from a prominent member of the community or land council supporting the application.

The use of any such material obtained from any of the above sources may be subject to restrictions imposed by the author or copyright provisions.

The Library of the Australian Institute of Aboriginal and Torres Strait Islander Studies is a storehouse of the records of Australian languages. Although it was only established in the 1960s, it contains much of the material on languages which was written before that. Even where material is not held by the Institute, a record in the computer catalogue will give the location of the institution holding the item.

Notes on works mentioned

Armstrong, FF 1871, Customs and Habits of Aborigines of Western Australia. In the Daisy Bates manuscript collection at the National Library of Australia. Ms 365 [Includes sentences in three Western Australian dialects]. His ms native vocabularies collected in 1837 are at Battye Library, Perth.

Backhouse, J 1832–1844, Manuscript journal. Mitchell Library. [Tasmanian material]

Barker, C, J Mulvaney and N Green 1992, *Commandant of Solitude: The Journals of Captain Collet Barker 1828–1831*, edited by John Mulvaney and Neville Green. Melbourne: Melbourne University Press at the Miegunyah Press. [Vocabulary and place names of Raffles Bay]

Bates, D 1900–1940, Papers. Canberra: National Library of Australia, Manuscript Section. Ms 365. Includes a guide to her papers. [Many Western Australian vocabularies collected as a result of a questionnaire she sent in 1904 to postmasters, police, farmers and settlers]

Bennett, JWO 1879, Vocabulary of the Woolner District Dialect, Adelaide River, Northern Territory. In JD Woods et al, *Native Tribes of South Australia*. Adelaide: ES Wigg.

Bunce, D 1851, *Language of the Aborigines of the Colony of Victoria and other Australian Districts*. Melbourne: Daniel Harrison.

Capell, A and HE Hinch 1970, *Maung Grammar, Texts and Vocabulary*. The Hague: Mouton.

Capell, A and HHJ Coate 1984, Comparative Studies in Northern Kimberley Languages, Australia, *Pacific Linguistics* C-69, Canberra.

Collins, D 1798–1802, *An Account of the English Colony in New South Wales, with Remarks on the Dispositions, Customs, Manners, etc. of the Native Inhabitants of that Country*. London: Cadell & W Davies. Another edition, edited by Brian H Fletcher. Sydney, Wellington: AH & AW Reed, 1975. [Includes Sydney vocabulary and comparisons between dialects]

Confalonieri, A 1846, Manner of Speaking or Short Conversation with the Natives of P. Essington, N. Australia. Photocopy at AIATSIS. [Iwaidja sentences]

Confalonieri, A 1847, Specimen of the Aboriginal Language or Short Conversation with the Natives of North Australia, Port Essington. Photocopy at AIATSIS. [Iwaidja sentences and vocabulary]

Curr, EM 1886–1887, *The Australian Race: Its Origin, Languages, Customs, Place of Landing in Australia and the Routes by Which It Spread Itself over that Continent*, 4 vols. Melbourne: Ferres.

Dawes, W 1790, Grammatical Forms of the Language of N.S. Wales in the Neighbourhood of Sydney. [Sydney]. Photocopy of ms at AIATSIS.

Dawes, W 1790, Vocabulary of the Language of N.S. Wales in the Neighbourhood of Sydney: Native and English but Not Alphabetical. [Sydney]. Photocopy of ms at AIATSIS.

Dawson, J 1881, *Australian Aborigines: The Languages and Customs of Several Tribes of Aborigines in the Western District of Victoria, Australia*. Melbourne: George Robertson. Facsimile edition, Canberra: Australian Institute of Aboriginal Studies, 1981. [Comparative vocabularies of Chaap wuurong, Kuurn kopan nook, Peek whuurong]

Dixon, RMW and BJ Blake (eds) 1979–, *Handbook of Australian Languages*. Canberra: Australian National University Press; and later Oxford University Press. [Grammatical sketches, phonology, vocabulary and sources for Guugu-Yimidhirr, Pitta-Pitta, Gumbaynggirr, Yaygir, Wargamay, Anguthimri, Watjarri, Margany, Gunya, Tasmanian, Djapu, Yukulta, Uradhi, Nyawaygi, Woiwurrung, Panyjima, Djabugay, Mbabaram]

Earl, GSW, 1853, *The Native Races of the Indian Archipelago: Papuans*. London: Bailliere. [Includes vocabularies of Port Essington area]

Elkin, AP 1923–1979, Papers. Sydney: University of Sydney Archives. [Includes vocabularies of Larrakia, Jawoyn in fieldnotes on Northern Territory tribes]

Grey, Sir G 1840, *A Vocabulary of the Dialects of South-western Australia,* 2nd edition. London: Boone.

Gunther, J 1892, Grammar and Vocabulary of the Aboriginal Dialect called the Wirradhuri. In LE Threlkeld, *An Australian Language as Spoken by the Awabakal.* Sydney: Stephens & Stokes. [Gunther's correspondence, 1829–1878 and notes on NSW Aborigines are held in the State Library of New South Wales, Sydney]

Hale, Horatio 1846, *United States Exploring Expedition during the Years 1838, 1839, 1840, 1841, 1842, under the Command of Charles Wilkes, USN: Ethnography and Philology.* Philadelphia: Lea and Blanchard. [Wiradjuri, Awabakal vocabulary and sentences]

Hoddinott, WG 1963–1982, Papers on the NSW North Coast, New England and Daly River (NT) Languages. Held at AIATSIS library.

Houzé, É and V Jacques 1884, *Étude d'anthropologie.* Bruxelles: F Hayez. [Includes vocabulary from Hinchinbrook Island]

Howitt, AW 1850–1906, Papers. Melbourne: held at the La Trobe Library. Copies of some papers at AIATSIS.

Jukes, JB 1847, *Narrative of the Surveying Voyage of HMS Fly, Commanded by Captain FP Blackwood, RN,* 2vols. London: T & W Boone. [Includes the language list by Evans of Hinchinbrook Island language]

Laves, G 1929–1932, Papers, mainly field notebooks, correspondence and language cards. Held at AIATSIS library. [Includes language notes, vocabulary and sentences for languages of NSW, South Australia, NT, Cape York and particularly Gumbaynggirr and Karajarri]

Lumholtz, C 1889, *Among Cannibals.* London: John Murray.

Lyon, R M 1833, A Glance at the Manners and Language of the Aboriginal Inhabitants of Western Australia, with a Short Vocabulary, *Perth Gazette* 1(13), 56; (14), 59–60; (15), 63–64; (16). Reprinted in N Green (ed) 1979, *Nyungar — The People.* Perth: Creative Research.

Mathews, RH [1880–1912?], [Australian languages material: fieldnotes]. [Phonologies, grammatical information and vocabulary for many languages particularly Victorian] AIATSIS Ms 3179. Also at AIATSIS are bound offprints of Mathews' published language material from many parts of Australia, particularly NSW and Victoria.

McCarthy, FD 1900–1945, [Aboriginal placenames, lists and related correspondence]. Manuscript at AIATSIS.

Meston, A 1891–1923, Papers. Brisbane: Oxley Library. [His lists of vocabularies from Aboriginal tribes include wordlists from many parts of Queensland and Northern NSW]

Meyer, HAE 1843, *Vocabulary of the Language Spoken by the Aborigines of South Australia Preceded by a Grammar.* Adelaide: Allen. [Vocabulary from Encounter Bay to Lake Alexandrina]

Milligan, Joseph 1878, On the Dialects and Language of the Aboriginal Tribes of Tasmania, and on their Manners and Customs. In RB Smyth, *The Aborigines of Victoria*, vol 2. Melbourne: Government Printer.

Moore, GF 1842, *A Descriptive Vocabulary of the Language in Common Use amongst the Aborigines of Western Australia.* London: Orr. Facsimile edition, Perth: University of Western Australia Press, 1978. [Vocabulary from Perth area, Vasse River and King Georges Sound]

Nekes, H and EA Worms 1953, *Australian Languages*. Fribourg: Anthropos-Institut. [Comprehensive study of Australian languages, particularly languages of the Kimberley Region, WA]

Parkinson, S 1773, *A Journal of a Voyage to the South Seas, in His Majesty's ship The Endeavour*. London. [Includes Banks' Guugu Yimithirr list]

Péron, F and L de Freycinet 1824, *Voyage de Découvertes aux Terres Australes*, vol 2, 2nd edition. Paris: Arthus Bertrand, Libraire. [Contains Tasmanian wordlists collected during Baudin expedition]

Ray, SH 1897, *Notes on the Languages of North-West Australia*. London: Harrison and Sons. [Located Brisbane: Oxley Library]

Ray, SH 1907, The Languages of the Torres Straits. In AC Haddon (ed), *Reports of the Cambridge Anthropological Expedition to the Torres Straits*, vol III. Cambridge: Cambridge University Press.

Reuther, JG 1928–1929, The Diari. Ms at South Australian Museum. Microfiche and electronic copy at AIATSIS. [Includes Diari dictionary, grammar of Diari, Jandruwanta and Wankanguru]

Ridley, WM 1875, *Kamilaroi and Other Australian Languages*, 2nd edition. Sydney: Government Printer. [As well as Kamilaroi, gives vocabulary, grammar and text from Brisbane River languages and others in NSW and Victoria]

Robinson, GA 1829–1844, Papers. Sydney: Mitchell Library. Microfilm copy at AIATSIS. [Vocabulary collected throughout Tasmania, and wordlists of southeastern Australian languages]

Rossel, EPE de 1808, Vocabulaire de la Langue d'une des Peuplades de la Terre de Van-Diémen. *Voyage de D'Entrecasteaux, Envoyé a la Recherche de La Pérouse.* Paris: L'Imprimerie Impériale. [Tasmanian wordlists obtained during D'Entrecasteaux Expedition]

Roth, WE 1897, *Ethnological Studies among the North-West Central Queensland Aborigines.* Brisbane: Government Printer. [Pitta-Pitta grammar and vocabulary]. Vocabularies of Dyirbal, Ngadjan, Ngikoongo, Gulngay, Yidiny, andGuugu-Yimithirr appeared in issues of North Queensland Ethnography Bulletins.

Salvado, R 1851, *Two Native Dialects of the New Norcia District.* Rome: De Propaganda Fides. Reprinted in EJ Stormon 1977, *The Salvado Memoirs.* Perth: University of Western Australia Press.

Schürmann, CW 1844, *Vocabulary of the Parnkalla Language Spoken by the Natives Inhabiting the Western Shores of Spencer's Gulf; to which is Prefixed a Collection of Grammatical Rules.* Adelaide: George Dehane.

Science of Man 1897–1913. Sydney: Anthropological Society of Australasia. Superseded *Australasian Anthropological Journal* 1896–1897.

Smyth, RB 1878, *The Aborigines of Victoria: with Notes Relating to the Habits of the Natives of other Parts of Australia and Tasmania,* 2 vols. Facsimile edition, Melbourne: John Currey O'Neill, 1972. [Collections of wordlists and lists of placenames]

Spencer, Sir WB 1880–1929, Papers. Sydney: Mitchell Library. [Includes an Arunta vocabulary] AIATSIS has copies of his papers held in National Museum of Victoria, Melbourne. [Includes Minyung, Larakya and Warrai language material]

Stanner, WEH 1933–1982, Papers. Held at AIATSIS library. [Included in the collection are linguistic materials from the Daly River area]

Strehlow, TGH 1944, *Aranda Phonetics and Grammar.* Sydney: Oceania Monographs.

Taplin, G 1879, *The Folklore, Manners, Customs and Languages of the South Australian Aborigines.* Adelaide: Government Printer. [Appendices contain grammar and vocabulary of Narrinyeri]

Teichelmann, CG and CW Schürmann 1840, *Outlines of a Grammar, Vocabulary, and Phraseology, of the Aboriginal Language of South Australia, Spoken by the Natives in and for Some Distance around Adelaide.* Adelaide: Authors.

Threlkeld, LE 1834, *An Australian Grammar, Comprehending the Principles and Natural Rules of the Language as Spoken by the Aborigines in the Vicinity of Hunter's River, Lake Macquarie, etc. New South Wales.* Sydney: Stephens & Stokes. Edition by John Fraser published in 1892. [Includes grammar, vocabulary, translations of St Luke's Gospel in Awabakal]. Threlkeld papers are in the Mitchell Library, Sydney.

Tindale, NB 1939–1963, Australian vocabularies [Fieldnotes]. Tindale Collection, South Australian Museum. [Vocabulary lists for 120 Australian languages]. AIATSIS has a copy of these vocabularies.

Walker, GW 1831–1849, Papers. Sydney: Mitchell Library.

Copyright

Copyright is a right of creators of literary, artistic, musical, dramatic works, films, sound recordings and some other creative work, which protects and encourages their creative and intellectual output. This right generally expires 50 years after the death of the author. Some of the published works mentioned in Chapter 3 are out of copyright, while others are not. Under the provisions of fair dealing for research or study, 10% of a book or an article in a periodical may be copied without infringing copyright.

If copyright material is going to be published, permission to publish must first be obtained from the copyright owner. The copyright holder is usually given with a © on the reverse of the title-page of a book. The publisher or the author of a journal article may hold copyright. If a book is out of print and unavailable, permission may be given by the publisher to copy the whole book.

The copyright laws have been primarily concerned with protecting material in a physical form, whether a book, photograph, or sound recording. The requirements for protecting the creative and intellectual work of people operating in an oral tradition have not yet been satisfactorily resolved. ■

 **Jaki Troy**

Reading old sources

 **Tamsin Donaldson**

What word is that?

4

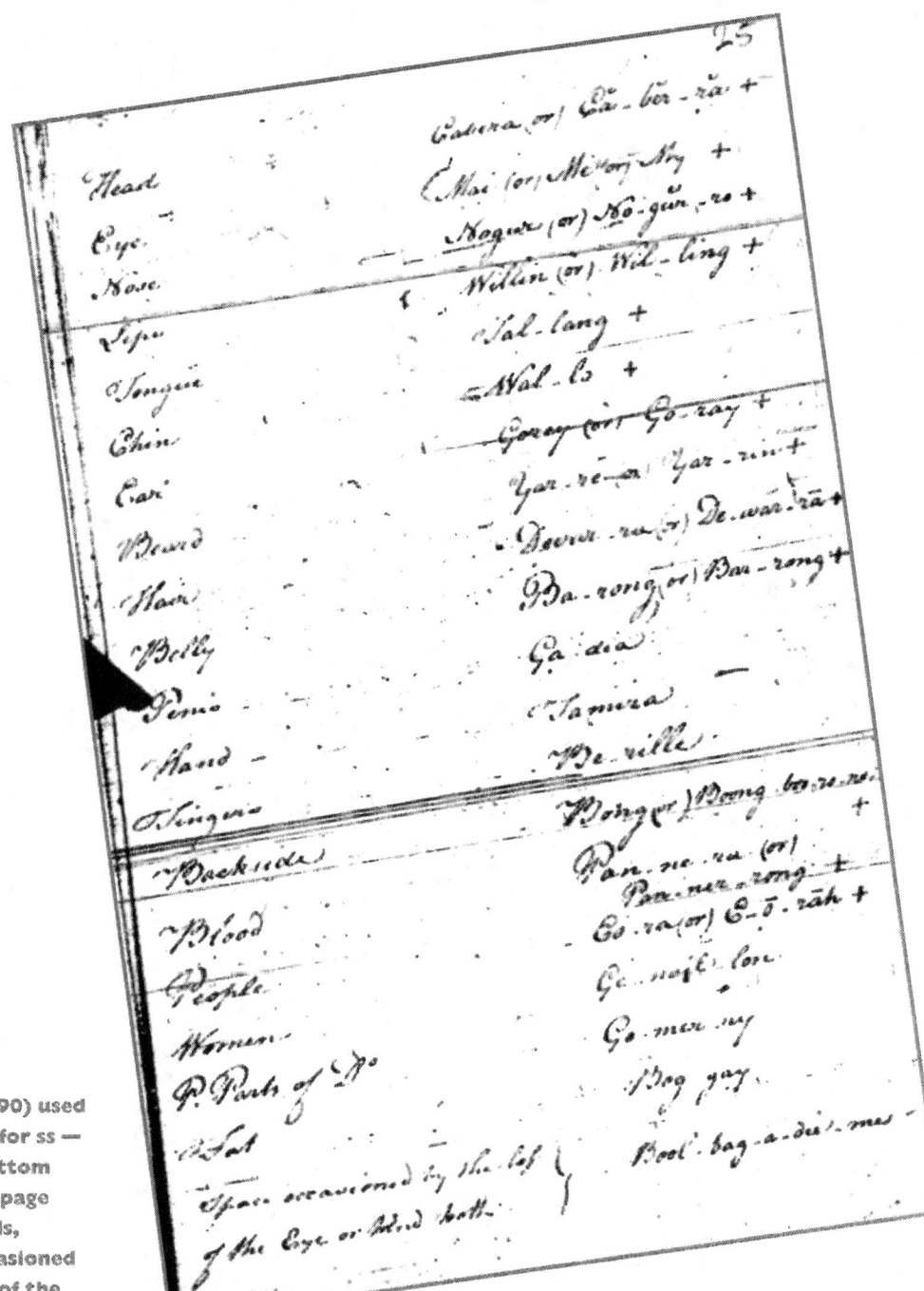

Head		Cadera (or) Cā-ber-ra +
Eye		Mai (or) Mi-ing Ny +
Nose		Nogur (or) No-gŭn-ro +
Lips		Willin (or) Wil-ling +
Tongue		Tal-lang +
Chin		Wal-lo +
Ear		Gorey (or) Go-ray +
Beard		Yar-re-in Yar-rin +
Hair		Deeure-ra (or) De-war-ra +
Belly		Ba-rong (or) Bar-rong +
Penis		Ga-dia
Hand		Tagura
Fingers		De-ville
Backside		Donger) Dong bo-re-ro
Blood		Pan-ne-ra (or) Pan-ner-rong +
People		Eo-ra (or) E-ō-rāh +
Women		Ge-nort-lon
P. Parts of Do		Go-mer-ny
Sat		Bog-gay
		Bool-bag-a-die-mes

Space occasioned by the lof)
of the Eye or blind both.

Dawes (1790) used the long ſ for ss — see the bottom left of the page which reads, 'Space occasioned by the loſ of the Eye or blind both'.

I have been working on the Sydney Language from old manuscript sources and have written a dictionary based on these sources (Troy 1994). A big problem in dealing with manuscripts, once you have found them, is reading the handwriting.

There are many kinds of records that could contain information about the language you want to research. Look for wordlists, handwritten and published, records to do with missions, transcripts of trials or reports to government inquiries. Library catalogues will not have what you want because they usually give broad descriptions of what is in the manuscript and may ignore brief reports of language names, conversations and so on. The catalogue may not list 'Aboriginal' or 'language' so you will need to look for other types of information such as names of missions or names of people who owned properties or businesses in the area. Often the property names have now become local placenames. Reading through nineteenth century novels can provide information, and may include local Aboriginal vocabulary. People's letters in archives often have useful cultural information as do journals from pastoral properties or military personnel.

Places to look for information include AIATSIS, the National Library of Australia, university libraries (especially those with specific manuscript collections) and local historical societies. (See Chapter 3 for more on sources of information.)

In the past the non-Aboriginal population used a lot of Aboriginal words that have gone out of general use now. In the First Fleet writings the words *badjagarang, bagaray, walaru, walaba* for types of kangaroo were used without translation, indicating that they were well known among the European settlers.

Because literacy was not widespread and the spelling system for English not highly regularised, spelling often reflected how people spoke. If you have a manuscript with spellings that do not make much sense to you, try pronouncing the words with different accents. If you know that the writer was Irish, for example, try saying the words with an Irish accent to see what they could represent.

Some old fashioned symbols were used in handwritten manuscripts. For instance, Threlkeld used *y* for the 'th' as in *ye* for 'the' and ∫ was commonly used for double *s* (see Dawes' use of ∫ in the bottom left of the illustration on page 36 which reads, 'Space occasioned by the lo∫ of the Eye or blind both').

From the late eighteenth century through to the mid-twentieth century copperplate writing was used. In the days before typewriters it was considered a quick and easy script for formal writing. Using copperplate, people would have a rough and a fair hand, one that was used for quick notes and scribblings, and the other used for more careful writing. Fair hand indicates that the material could have been copied from somewhere else and if it is in alphabetical order it is likely that more careful attention has been paid to the data. An example of rough and fair hand can be seen in the example below, a manuscript from 1790, in which the rough hand is that of Arthur Philip, first Governor of New South Wales. The example at the bottom of the page shows Dawes' fair hand used in a page of well-organised information.

The rough and fair copperplate hands can be clearly distinguished in this 1790 manuscript. The example below shows the organised fair hand of Dawes.

Copperplate used the nibs of ink pens to give wide and narrow strokes on letters. This can make it hard to read as the wide downstrokes could be quite dark in comparison to the lighter upstrokes, and the inks have faded, leaving only the darker lines on the page. Sometimes people would write both ways to save paper. In addition, inks bleed over time, so that some manuscripts are virtually unreadable today.

An example of a copperplate hand from *The Art of Writing* by Charles Snell, 1712.

'Tis very advantagious for ingenious men to communicate their sentiments to each other it discovers a generosity improves the judgement invigorates the fancy creates emulation and promotes industry

Look at the example on the next page which shows William Dawes' key to his spelling system. Dawes was one of the earliest recorders of an Aboriginal language, in this case the Sydney Language. This is his own spelling system and we can only guess what he meant by some of the symbols or diacritics (marks above or below the letter) such as a dot above or beside *a*. His own accent, from the south of England and London of the late eighteenth century, gives some clues. Note also the use of ŋ which began in the seventeenth century. Peter Austin and Terry Crowley discuss interpretation of handwriting and printing errors on pages 86–87.

William Dawes' manuscript explaining the key to his spelling.

Letter	Name	Sound	As in the english words
à	aw	aw	all call
a	a	a	at am an
b	be	b	
d	de	d	
e	e	e	ell empty
f			
g	gay	g hard	good gum
h			
i	ĕ	ĕ	in it ill
ai	aí	aí	I ivy ire
k	ka	k	
l	el	l	
m	em	m	
n	en	n	
ŋ	eng	ng	sing king
o	o	o	open over
p	pe	p	
r	er	r	
s	es	s	
t	te	t	
u	os	oo	cool fool
u	a	u	un- under
z			

The poor legibility of many manuscripts is the result of a combination of the factors discussed above, and to make them useful today it is usual to transcribe them carefully, marking on your transcript where the writing is not legible, and creating typed files, on a computer, which can then be searched and treated like other computer-based information. This process is discussed in more detail in Chapter 9. ■

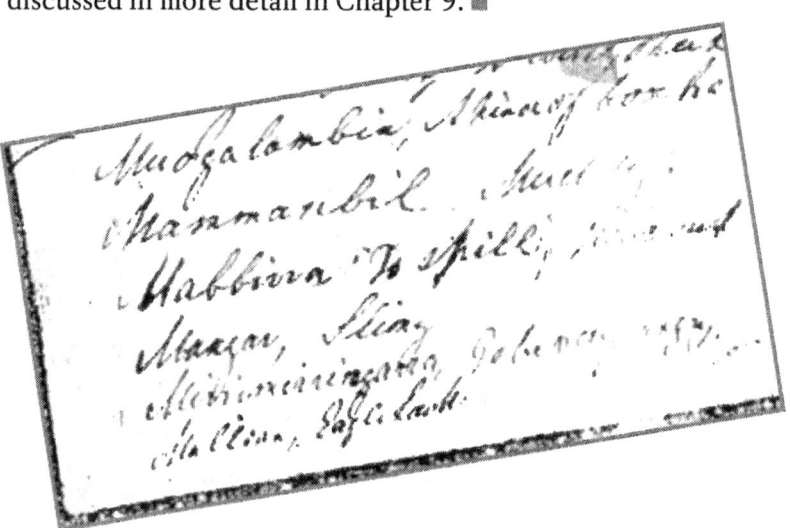

Günther's Wiradjuri wordlist. The word in the third line from the bottom was mistyped as 'sling' instead of 'slimy'.

hy is it so hard for us today to read so many of the language words that were first written down?

**What word
is that?
A hearing
writing
reading
game**

Here is a game to help us understand what the people who first tried to write down words from Aboriginal languages were up against. This is important because then we can make better sense of what they wrote. We also have a better chance of getting round some of their difficulties when we start writing language words ourselves. We start out facing many of the same problems now, especially if, like most of them, we aren't used to hearing or speaking ancestral languages and are — so far — only used to reading and writing English.

This simple experiment allows us to share some of the frustrations of the early writers — and have a laugh on the way to solutions.

To play it you will need plenty of slips of paper, a container to hold them, and one person among you who can speak a suitable word of his or her language, or a tape-recording of the word. The results will be most interesting if the language, or at least the word, is one that none of the rest of you know already, and also if the word is a longish one. There are two parts to the game.

veryone listens to the word being spoken, or played on tape, just a couple of times, and then writes what they hear on a slip. You each write it down as best you can, whatever way you like, without discussing amongst yourselves or getting

Part one

repeat pronunciations from the speaker. (Captain Cook and Joseph Banks, the first writers of the first Australian language word to get into English, 'kangaroo', wrote down 'kanguru', 'kanguroo' and 'kangooroo' to represent what they had heard Guugu Yimithirr speakers say in mid-1770, then sailed away on the *Endeavour* without any opportunity to go back for later checks.) What you are thinking about and aiming at as you write is how to help yourself remember exactly what you heard, and how to help other people to know exactly what you heard, so that later you and other people will be able to say it the same way with only the writing and not the voice to help you.

Put your slip (or slips if you want to give it more than one try) into the container, and have a break; do something else for a bit. This is to let your memories of the spoken word fade before testing the written versions.

Part two   ass round the container, and everybody take a turn to pick a slip (not your own). You can ask some more people who weren't involved in the first part to join in at this point if you like. Have a go at reading your slip aloud for everyone to hear. Then hold it up for everyone else to see, so that anyone who thinks there's another obvious way to read it can have a go at reading it aloud too. How many people have written down the word the same way? And how many ways of reading each spelling did you come up with?

Ivan Couzens
(Gunditj Mara) has
picked a spelling
of a Guugu
Yimithirr word to
test what
pronunciation it
produces.

At the end you can ask the speaker to say the word again or you can play the recording some more. Did any of the readings of any of your spellings make you say exactly what the speaker said? If so, congratulations! You have been lucky! But it's equally likely that you have not been lucky, and that NONE of your readings from any of your spellings have produced the speaker's way of saying the word. Do not be downhearted; this is NORMAL! Don't throw the slips away; list the different spellings where you can look at them all next to one another, like Terry Crowley and Peter Austin do with the different old spellings of Bundjalung and Gamilaraay words in Chapter 5.

GYSGURRUNGU

BAJARANGAL

GU A CANGARA

gaygarrgu

Gi GAA RAAN GU

GAGAGARNGAL

GIGURANGGUR

gai garangu

GUNGURRUNGOO

gigarungul

GANGARANGOO

GAYGURRANGGURR

GHIGURAANGU

GOA-KARUNGU

Ka KARUNGOO

GAAGARANGU

Gagardangoo

GUYCANr

Gurriegurangoo

Gygarangu

KARLGARUNGU

KAI KAI KARANGr

Look at the
different spellings
next to one
another.

This is where the game gets to be really useful. You can learn a lot of things from looking at all your results together, whether any of them were successful for getting back the word the speaker said or not. There are several different kinds of things to discover:

- There is strength in numbers of different spellings. By comparing them you may be able to work out what the original word was, even if none of the spellings on their own will help you to the original pronunciation and only the original pronunciation (as shown for Bundjalung words in Chapter 5).

- You can learn exactly which are the new sounds for English speakers to hear and to say, to write and to read. You will also notice how often people used to writing and reading English tend to read some letters and combinations of letters differently according to what other letters there are in the word.

- You can learn that there is a method for getting around all the mismatches between the systems of sounds used in Aboriginal languages and the sound system of English. There is a method for getting around the limitations of English ways of using the alphabet to write and read English when it comes to using the same alphabet to write and read Aboriginal languages. The method is to start with the sound system of the Aboriginal language, decide on a letter or combination of letters to represent each sound and stick with writing it that way every time that sound comes up. If a person approaches a word of the language written your way as if it were an English word, they may still not read it successfully. But if you also provide a key to your writing system, if they are not successful in reading it how you want them to, it will be because they haven't given your system a go.

The illustration on page 46 shows the slips from the time the participants in the Paper and Talk workshop played this game. The word we know in English as 'kangaroo' comes from the Guugu Yimithirr word for one kind of kangaroo — a large blackish one. The word we experimented with writing down was another Guugu Yimithirr word for another kind of kangaroo — a smaller one that lives in rocky country higher up.

Here is the Guugu Yimithirr word as written in the spelling system used for the language today by the Guugu Yimithirr people of Hopevale in Queensland:

galgaranggurr

Here is a key to the sounds of the letters when they are used for writing Guugu Yimithirr:

g	between English *k* and *g*
a	like *u* in English cut
l, r	as in English
u	like *u* in English put

ng   like *ng* in English singer

rr   like a Scottish *r*, but quite quiet at the end of a word

The letters represent the same sounds in the spelling system (orthography) used for Guugu Yimithirr as they do in the spelling systems used for Bundjalung, Gamilaraay and Kaurna (see 'Letters, sounds and how to say them' on pp 111–13).

Let us now return to Captain Cook's, Sir Joseph Banks' and today's spellings of 'kangaroo'. According to the Guugu Yimithirr spelling system they write their word *gangurru*. If we follow the key we can find out how they pronounce it. If Guugu Yimithirr people wanted to make people say the English speakers' pronunciation of 'kangaroo' that we have got used to reading and saying from our spelling, and from Cook's and Banks' that led to it, they would write 'ganggaru', to make us say that extra *g*-sound after the *ng*-sound.

The final illustration is 'Different readings of different ways of writing the (Guugu Yimithirr word) *galgaranggurr*'. On three occasions when 'What word is that?' was played, I tape-recorded the ways in which people read out the slips they picked, together with alternative readings suggested by other players who disagreed with the first reading. So that you can have an impression of how the game went, I have typed out the slips and transcribed the ways they were read, using the 'International Phonetic Alphabet (IPA) symbols for use in Australian English' which are listed with a pronunciation key at the front of the

Macquarie Dictionary. I used *rr* from the Guugu Yimithirr spelling system as well, because Australian English does not have that sound. You will notice that no-one was game to try reading one of the spellings! And that there was only one spelling that was used by more than one person. Among all the spellings, only one found a reader who read it so that it sounded to Frankie Deemal like his own original word — and that was because both writer and reader had had some helpful previous experience in hearing, saying, writing and reading Aboriginal languages. After the game, everybody had had some!

The first occasion was an AIATSIS History Workshop. Guugu Yimithirr participant Frankie Deemal said the word *galgaranggurr* (and did not make a slip or read aloud other people's). A number of the other participants already had some familiarity with spelling systems in use for other Aboriginal languages, usually their own. The second group were workshopping problems to do with deciding on spelling systems to use for their own languages — Narrunga, Ngarrindjeri and Kaurna. The third group were mainly educators interested in literacy in English. Some knew and could read and write some other languages, including Italian and Turkish, but few knew anything about Aboriginal languages.

Different readings of different ways of writing *galgarangurr*

AIATSIS History Workshop

1	kulkadrnungnu	(No-one tried to read this one)
2	kacarangua	[ˈkʌtʃə ˌrʌŋʊwʌ] [ˈkæekə ˌrænguw]
3	kulkarungoo	[kʊlkəˈrʌŋʊ] [kʊlkʌˈrʊŋʊ]
4	kalkarungkurr	[ˈkælkərʊŋ ˌkʊr]
5	kullakurunguu	[ˈkʌləkə ˌrʌŋgu] [ˈkʊlʌkə ˌrʊŋʊ]
6	cukarungoo	[ˈkʊkə ˌrʊŋgu]
7	kalkarr'anggur	[ˈkʊlkə ˌraŋʊə] [kælkəˈræŋʊr]
		[kælˈkærʊŋgʊr]
8	kalarunlul	[ˈkælə ˌrʊnlʊl]
9	kalkarunggurr	[ˈkælkərʊŋ ˌgurr]
10	kurlgarungoo	[ˈkʊəlkərʌŋu]
11	kulkarunggurr	[ˈkʊlkʌrʊ ˌŋurr]
12	kalkarungu	[ˈkælkʌrʊŋu] [ˈkælkərʊŋʊ]
13	kalkarungal	[ˌkælkərʊŋˈgʌl]
14	kalkarangkurr	(Read like a Guugu Yimithirr person says *galgarangurr*)
15	kalkarungurr	[ˌkalkaruˈŋuər]
16	kulkarungurr	[ˌkalkarʌŋˈgərr]
17	kalkarangu	[ˌkalkaraˈŋu]
18	kukulrangoodt	[kʊkʊlˈrʌŋut]
19	kulkarungurr	[ˌkulkʌrʊˈŋuərr]

These phonetic transcriptions show how people at three different workshops read the Guugu Yimithirr word *galgarangurr* from slips of paper which they had written earlier in the day. Note how many different ways of reading this word there are. For a key to the phonetic symbols look at the front of the *Macquarie Dictionary*.

Adelaide Local Languages Course
Kura Yerlo Centre

I	gulgarangu	[ˌɡʌlɡəˈræŋɡʌ] [ˌɡʌlɡəˈræŋɡʊ] [ˈɡʊlɡəˌraɲʊ]
2	gulkarungu	[ˌkʊlkəˈrʌŋɡu] [kʊlkəˈrʊŋɡu]
3	kalkarngu	[kælˈkaŋɡu]
4	galkarrangu	[ˌɡælkəˈræɲu] [ɡʌlkəˈræɲu]
5	kalgangru	[ˌkʌlˈkʌŋɡrʊ]
6	kulgarangu	[ˌkʊlkəˈrænyʊ] [kʊlkəˈræŋɡʊ] [ˌkʊlkəˈrʌɲʊ]
7	kalkarrangkurr	[ˈkʌlkaˌræŋɡʊr]
8	karkarrangkur	[ˈkʌrkaˌrʌŋɡur]

Future of Literacy Symposium
Bond University

I	kulkarandor	[ˈkʌlkəˌrændɔ] [kʊlkərænˈdɔ] [ˈkʊlkəˌrʌndɔ]
2	kulkurgood	[ˈkʌlkəˌɡʊd] [kʊlˈkʊəˌɡʊd]
3	galgarangur	[ˌɡælɡəˈræŋɡə] [ɡʌlɡəˈrʌŋɡʊə]
4	gulgarangul	[ˌɡʌlɡəˈræŋɡʊl] [ɡʌlɡəˈrʌŋɡʊl]
5	galgarunguk	[ɡʌlɡəˈræŋɡʌk] [ɡʌlɡəˈrʊŋɡʊk] [ɡælɡəˈrʌŋɡʌk]
6	galgarungul	[ˈɡʌlɡərʌŋɡəl]
7	galgarangur	(same as 3, not read again)
8	kalkarangur	[ˌkælkəˈræŋɡə]
9	gancuyar	[ɡanˈkuyʌ][ˈɡæŋkuya] [ɡaɲˈkuyʌ] [ɡʌnˈsuya]
10	calcarungur	[ˈkælkəˌrʌŋɡə] [kælˈkʌrɪŋɡʊər] [ˌkælkʌrʌɲˈɡʊə]

Peter Austin

Terry Crowley

Interpreting old spelling

Looking at old spelling

I n this chapter we are going to look at ways of 'reconstituting' pronunciation and correct spelling of words that are to be found in old written sources. We will show you some methods for working with old documents to sort out how old spellings can be interpreted. However, you must remember that reconstitution can only be as good as the sources that it is based on; if the spelling in the sources is poor then our reconstitution will be affected by this, and you will not be able to come up with very accurate interpretations. Sometimes, it will even be necessary to say, 'We don't know what sounds the writer is trying to represent — it could be this, or it could be that', or even, 'We simply can't tell'. It is important to be honest about this from the beginning and to recognise the limitations that face us when we try to work with old spellings. This doesn't mean that we should give up and not try to interpret the materials we have available; rather, that we must be realistic and accept that, like reconstituted orange juice, the language can never sound as good as the original did.

Spelling and pronunc- iation

D ifferent people pronounce words in any language in different ways. In the same way, different people sometimes have different ways of spelling words. Why is this so?

Differences in pronunciation can arise for a number of reasons. Sometimes, people who speak the same language come from different places, so we say that they speak different dialects of that language. They can understand one another pretty well, but sometimes they choose to use a different word or expression, or sometimes they may use the same word but pronounce it slightly differently. We are familiar with this in English: people from Australia speak differently from people from England (and even within England there are lots of regional variations), and people from both places speak differently from people in America (again, there is lots of regional variation to be found in America).

The same is true for Aboriginal languages. For example, the word that we write in English as 'Koori' is derived from a word that originally just meant 'man' in the language of the Sydney area, and some of the languages along the coast to the north of Sydney, as far as Kempsey. In these languages, some people used to say *guri*, while others used to say *kuri*. It wouldn't have mattered, from the point of view of understanding one another, which pronunciation somebody used, since both were perfectly acceptable to speakers of all of these languages at the time. When we come to spell words that vary in their pronunciation like this, our main aim is going to be consistency, so that spelling reflects pronunciation in a consistent way.

Sometimes differences in pronunciation can be purely personal, as with a person who has a lisp, or someone who swallows their sounds when they speak. Again, we have to be careful to recognise this and to aim for a spelling that represents the most common pronunciation and one that all people will recognise and understand.

When you work with written source materials and try to figure out the original pronunciations of old words, you will notice immediately that different people have written the same words in different ways. Why is this?

For English, correct spelling is taken to be a sign of literacy and a good education, but not many people realise that it was only in the last few hundred years that spelling became so strict as it is now. It was only when English dictionaries became widely available, and spelling was taught in school, that it became possible to say that one spelling was 'correct' and another 'incorrect'. Before that, people often spelled words in different ways (and sometimes one person spelled the same word differently, as the mood took them), adding a letter here or a letter there, or leaving them out as they liked. Sometimes printers did this to make up the length of lines in books. It didn't matter much as long as everyone was still able to read what was written, and understand what was meant.

When it comes to spelling words in a foreign language, as Aboriginal languages were to almost all the early writers, there are a number of extra reasons why we might find different spellings in the written records that are available to us. One of these is the writer's own language background (whether they spoke English, or French, as their main language, for example), and even their dialect (working class northern English versus educated southern English). We will discuss this in more detail later. Another reason could be the length of time they spent learning the language. We might reasonably expect that someone who had spent many years living in a community (such as a teacher or missionary) might have a better grasp of the language and be able to spell words better than someone who had just visited for a day or so, like a passing traveller. We might also expect that a person who has lived in or visited several different communities, or who had tried to learn several languages, might be better placed to respond to language differences. This isn't always true, but we must keep it in mind and look into the background of the person who wrote down the words we are trying to make sense of, including where he or she lived and where they travelled to.

Another reason we might find spelling differences is the general level of interest in language and culture shown by the person who collected the information. Someone who is more sympathetic to Aboriginal people and culture is more likely to spend the time to learn the language properly and to try to spell it more accurately. Individual differences play a large part here: some collectors were just more careful and tried harder to be accurate than others did.

Looking at source materials in archives such as those at AIATSIS shows that there are many different spelling systems in use by language collectors. When trained linguists write words in Aboriginal languages, they use a special (phonetic) alphabet that makes it possible to clearly indicate exactly how a word is pronounced. When other linguists trained to use the same symbols look at how a word has been written, they know immediately how it should be pronounced.

Many of you will have seen books written about Aboriginal languages in which a number of strange-looking symbols might occur. Words written using these symbols might look something like this (see for example the phonetics used on pp 51–52) :

ŋ ʒ ɜ ð ɾ θ ˢ ɹ œ ɫ ɶʒ ɖ ɟ

While linguists know how to interpret spellings such as these, people who have not been trained in linguistics often cannot make much sense out of what has been written.

This means that when we write languages that have not been written before by their speakers, we need to have a more practical way of spelling them, which only uses letters of the alphabet that ordinary people are familiar with. The spelling system that is adopted for any particular language will always depend in the end on how the people with an inherited interest in the language want to write it themselves.

At the same time, there are several important principles that people have to keep in mind when a writing system is being developed for a language. The most important principle is that the same sound should always be represented in the same way in the spelling system in whatever word it occurs in. This means that when we write a language we should not represent a *k*-sound sometimes as *k* , and at other times as *c* or even as *ck*.

By using the same spelling for the same sound, we are making sure that there can never be any confusion about how a word is to be pronounced. For instance, if a word that is pronounced *maka* were to be written by one person as *maka* and by another person as *maca*, a third person trying to read the same words would not be sure if these two spellings were meant to represent one pronunciation, or two different pronunciations.

We have shown you elsewhere in this manual some of the kinds of decisions that have been made about spelling different Aboriginal languages in Australia, so we will not go into any more detail at this point about how a spelling system could be devised for your language if it does not already have one.

The important point to keep in mind is that very few of the published and unpublished sources on the languages that you will be dealing with were written by people with training in linguistics. The vast majority of the people who were writing words in Aboriginal languages in the nineteenth century, and even in most of the early part of the twentieth century, were English speakers who were hearing the sounds of Aboriginal languages through the sounds of English that they already knew, and who were writing these sounds with the spelling system that they had already learned in school for English.

A smaller number of people who were speakers of other European languages wrote words in Aboriginal languages as well, especially speakers of French and German. When these people wrote words in Aboriginal languages, they would have heard the sounds through the sounds of their own languages, and they would have written them down following the spelling rules of their own languages, as in the case study of Ngarla (see Chapter 9) where the recorder was Italian.

Because of this fact, it is important to pay attention to the language background of the person who was writing your ancestral language. The same spelling given by a speaker of German, or of French, or of English, might have been intended to represent quite different things. In fact, even speakers of different varieties of English may have used different sorts of spellings to represent the same sounds, depending on how they pronounced words in their own dialect of English.

Information sources

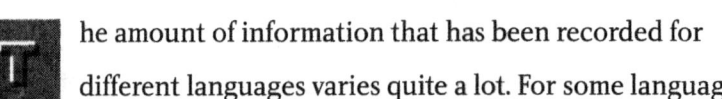he amount of information that has been recorded for different languages varies quite a lot. For some languages we might have only one or two wordlists, and for others there can be many vocabularies available. It is important to realise that there can be errors in the wordlists that collectors took down. Several sorts of errors can creep in, especially when the collector was not properly trained and did not spend a great deal of time studying the language. From our own work, and that of linguists like Luise Hercus and Gavan Breen, we can identify the following types of errors as being common:

- misunderstanding what a word in an Aboriginal language meant

- mixing words from several different languages together in a single list
- mistakes in spelling words

We will look at each of these in turn.

Firstly, misunderstanding the meanings of words is not uncommon in old sources, especially when the collector and interviewee had no language in common and must have relied on gestures and pointing. Sometimes, the meaning given in a wordlist is completely wrong because the collector did not understand the English spoken by the Aboriginal person who gave them the words. In early days, Aboriginal people's English was often heavily accented and showed the effect of the languages they spoke. This can be seen in the following examples taken from wordlists that we have examined:

Wordlist meaning	Correct meaning
heart	hot
wet	sweat
moths	boss
shit, dung	tongue

Sometimes, the Aboriginal person may have given the correct English word, and pronounced it correctly as well. However, if it was a word that has more than one meaning in English, the collector may have thought the word referred to a different thing. For instance, there is an example where an Aboriginal person said that a particular word meant 'bark', which the collector took to mean 'bark of a tree'. In fact, however, the

Aboriginal person was referring to the barking of dogs, and the word should have been translated as 'bark' or 'make a sound'.

Another problem is that sometimes a specific term is translated for a general term, or a general term is given when a specific term was meant. Here are some examples:

Wordlist meaning	Correct meaning
grass	vegetation
boy	uninitiated youth
beard	hair
day	now
thumb	your hand
girl	female
snake	carpet snake

Finally, we sometimes find a meaning listed for a word which is actually that of a related word; this is especially true where pointing and gestures would have been used. Here are some examples:

Wordlist meaning	Correct meaning
thighs	buttocks
cloud	sky
woman	wife
hair	head
ground	camp
frown	blind
spider	to bite
dig	drink

You can imagine how the last two came about — the collector points at an insect and says 'spider', while the Aboriginal person giving words says, 'Look out. It will bite'. For the last example, the collector could have said, 'Dig the ground', perhaps making the motions of scratching a hole in the ground, and the Aboriginal person thinks, 'Poor fellow. He's thirsty and is digging a soakage for a drink!'

Mixing words from different Aboriginal languages in vocabulary lists is something that we must be careful of and try to look out for. Sometimes, it can even look as if a wordlist belongs to just one language, while what has really happened is just that the writer has thrown together words from a variety of different languages into a single list for some reason! Some Europeans also seem to have believed that all Aboriginal languages were somehow the same, so it was alright to put together words that they gathered from different places into single lists.

One other common mistake of this kind was the recording of some of the pidgin English words that were widely used in the past as if they were words in a particular local language. Words like *bindji* for 'stomach', or *coolamon* for 'dish', spread out from Sydney with the early settlers and these words sometimes appear in vocabularies from other areas instead of the original words for these things.

Finally, there can be mistakes in the written sources because of problems with spelling words. We cover these in the next section.

Comparing information

hen we have two or more written sources we can compare the spellings and meanings of words given to come up with guesses about what the language was probably like. Generally speaking, the greater the amount of recorded information, the greater the amount of inconsistency there seems to be in how words were recorded. It often seems that there were as many different ways for people to spell the same word as there were people who were trying to write it!

While it might seem like a nuisance that there is so much variation in people's spellings of words in Aboriginal languages, we should, in fact, regard this inconsistency as our friend, rather than our enemy. Very often, the fact that people have given us different spellings can point to the exact sound that they were trying to represent, but which they were having so much trouble with. We can compare the different spellings to get at the most likely original pronunciation.

Let us take a simple example first of all. A number of different sources from the 1800s and early 1900s have written the word for 'man' in Bundjalung (which comes from the northern coast of New South Wales, and extends into parts of southern Queensland) like this:

bygul   beigal   bigal   bygle   bycol   baygul

In this case, we are lucky because there are still lots of people living in Lismore and surrounding areas who can tell us how the Bundjalung word for 'man' is actually pronounced. These pronunciations tell us that the correct spelling should be *baygal.*

So, how is it that these earlier observers managed to write this word in so many different ways, with not a single spelling being correct? The answer is that these people were all English speakers, and they tried to interpret the pronunciation of the word *baygal* as if it were an English word. They then tried to represent their interpretation of the sound by spelling it as if it were an English word.

The first part of the Bundjalung word is spelt *bay-*, and it sounds very much like the English word 'by', as in 'the man sat by his wife'. The same sound in English can also be spelt as 'bi', in a word such as 'biting'. That is why many of the early recorders wrote the word beginning with 'by-', while some others represented this sound as 'bi-'.

In Bundjalung, it does not make any difference in a word like *baygal* whether you make the sound *a* or *e*. (In this respect, Bundjalung is very similar to many other Aboriginal languages.) Because it does not matter if people actually pronounce *ay* (as in English 'eye') or *ey* (as in English 'ray'), it is best to write these sounds all the same, and the Bundjalung have agreed to write *ay*.

Some of the people who wrote this word in these early sources clearly heard an *ey*-sound. In one of these words, 'beigal' you can see that the person tried to represent this as 'ei'. The spelling 'baygul' was perhaps also meant to represent the same sound, with the first part of the word rhyming with the English words 'bay' and 'ray'.

If we turn our attention to the middle of the word, you will see that most people have written a *g*, while one person has written a *c*. The letter *c* in English is often used to represent a *k*-sound, as in words like 'can' or 'because'. In very many Aboriginal languages (including Bundjalung) it does not make any difference whether we pronounce a *g* or a *k*, so these two sounds should be represented by the same spelling wherever they occur. In the spelling system that has been agreed on for Bundjalung, these sounds are both written as *g*.

The very last letter of this word is written in most sources as *l*, so it seems to be fairly certain that these people were all trying to write a word that ends in the sound *l*. The spelling 'bygle' might seem a little puzzling, but in fact many words that end in the sound *l* in English are spelt with *-le* at the end:

rifle	little
wriggle	puzzle

So far, we have been able to show that this word should be reconstituted as having begun with *bayg-* and as ending in *-l*. But we still have not shown what has happened with the sound that occurs between the *g* and the *l*. The spellings that have been recorded seem to vary quite a lot. Some sources give us 'a', some give us 'o', while others give us 'u'.

The spelling 'bygle' makes it look like the sound between the *g* and the *l* was the same indistinct sort of sound that we find before the final sound in words like 'rifle', 'little', 'wriggle', 'puzzle' and so on. This indistinct sound is the same sound that is represented in a variety of different ways in English spelling:

total	wretched
cannon	awful
putrid	

What happens in Bundjalung (as well as many other Australian languages) is that the sounds *a, i* and *u* all often end up sounding a bit like this indistinct sound in English when there is more emphasis placed on another part of the word. In Bundjalung, there is greater emphasis placed on the first part of the word, ie on *bay-*, while the second half of the word gets swallowed up a little bit.

But if you listen very carefully, or if you get a speaker of Bundjalung to pronounce the word very slowly, you will hear that this indistinct sound is really meant to be an *a*-sound. This means that on the basis of all of these alternative spellings, we could settle on the correct spelling for this word as *baygal*. And, of course, we are lucky enough in this case to have Bundjalung people who can still pronounce the word, and we can see that this is in fact the correct spelling.

This demonstration shows that when there are a number of different spellings of a word in old sources, what you should do is compare these spellings against one another. One easy way to do this is to line up spellings above one another and compare the letters that were used to write the words. Here are these old spellings once again lined up in the kind of way that we mean:

b	ay	g	u	l
b	y	g	u	l
b	ei	g	a	l
b	i	g	a	l
b	y	g		le
b	y	c	o	l
b	**ay**	**g**	**a**	**l**

Common spelling errors

ere is an example of another set of spellings lined up in the same way, this time the word for 'ear', so we can see how the correct pronunciation of this word can be worked out. The correct spelling as provided by speakers of Bundjalung is given under the line at the bottom:

p	e	n	u	ng
b	i	n	u	ng
b	i	nn	u	ng
p	i	n	a	ng
b	i	n	o	ng
b	**i**	**n**	**a**	**ng**

The first thing that you should note is that the spellings 'b' and 'p' at the beginning of this word point to the same kind of variation as we found in the middle of the word *baygal*. Just as *g* and *k*-sounds in Aboriginal languages are often interchangeable, the difference between *b* and *p* generally does not need to be represented in the spelling systems for these languages. The spelling system that has been adopted for Bundjalung represents both of these sounds as *b*.

You should note that double letters like *nn* in the middle of a word in English generally show that the previous vowel is short, and not that the doubled letter itself is pronounced double. This means that a spelling like 'binnung' is probably meant to be pronounced with a short *i* like in the word 'dinner'. If it had been a single *n*, the sound might have been the longer sound that we find in the English word 'diner'.

In the spelling 'bigal' for the previous word, all of the sources write the middle sound with only one *g*, which indicates that the preceding letter is meant to be pronounced with a sound like the *i* in 'fine'. If the word for 'man' were meant to be pronounced 'bigal' rather than *baygal*, we would have expected the old sources to give spellings something like 'biggal' or 'biggle'.

You can see that one of the sources has spelt the word for 'ear' as 'penung', in which the first part of the word contains an 'e' spelling rather than an 'i' spelling. Aboriginal languages generally only have three vowel sounds — *a*, *i* and *u*. Where you find variation in spellings between *i* and *e*, the correct spelling is probably *i*.

Similarly, when there is variation in spellings between *a* and *o*, the correct spelling is probably *a*. In this example, you can see that there are spellings that show this kind of variation, such as 'pinang' and 'binong'. These suggest that the word should be written as *binang*. The spellings that contain 'u' before the final 'ng', such as 'binnung', are also consistent with this pronunciation, as the letter *u* in English, when it is followed by a consonant (or a group of consonants) at the end of a word, is often used to represent a similar sort of sound in English:

but   sung   crust

What we will do now is show you a list of many of the different kinds of spellings that are often used by speakers of English when they are writing words in Aboriginal languages. One of the problems is that often the same letter can be used to represent a number of different sounds in the Aboriginal language, so unless you are able to check some pronunciations out with some older people who still remember some of the language, it may not be possible to be certain about the exact original pronunciation at all.

Vowel sounds

We will begin with the vowel sounds (see the table opposite). You will remember that we said it was important to consider what a person's own language background is when you are working out how to interpret old spellings. If you come across a spelling like *u* in many English words, it is not always possible to be sure whether this is meant to represent the sound *u* or *a*, because the letter *u* can be pronounced as in the word 'put', or as in the word 'but'.

Spelling	Possible pronunc-iation	Comment	Examples	Correct spelling
a, ar	*a*	in the middle of a word	parneh	**bana**
er, ah, eh	*a*	at the end of a word	parneh	**bana**
a	*ay*	when there is a single consonant followed by a vowel	pana	**bayna**
e	*i*		pena	**bina**
	a	especially after *y, dj* or *ny*	jena	**djana**
i, ee, ie	*i*		peenar	**bina**
ea	*i*	following *y* or *dj*	yealki	**yilgi**
i	*ay*	when there is a single consonant followed by a vowel, especially *e*	biner	**bayna**
y	*ay*	when there is a single consonant followed by a vowel	bynah	**bayna**
	i	especially at the end of a word	pyny	**bayni**
o	*u*		poonah	**buna**
	a	especially after *w*	woner	**wana**
u, oo	*u*		puna	**buna**
u	*a*	when there is a double consonant after it in the middle of a word, or a single consonant at the end of a word	punnah	**bana**

But, if you have two different people recording a word, one an English person who writes *u*, and another a French person who writes *ou*, then it is likely that the sound should have been *u* rather than *a*. The reason for this is that the letters *ou* in French are only ever used to spell the sound *u*, and never *a*. The word *bouche* in French, which means 'mouth', is pronounced very much like the English word 'bush'. If a French person wanted to write a word that sounds like English 'rush', it would look quite different — probably something like *rache*.

Some Aboriginal languages make a difference between long vowels and short vowels; long vowels are drawn out in their pronunciation, and they are written double. This can make quite a meaning difference, as in the following words from Gamilaraay:

tharra	'thigh'	**tharraa**	'drunk'
guway	'blood'	**guwaay**	'is speaking'
garril	'leaf'	**gariil**	'cold'

Unfortunately, it is very difficult to distinguish long and short vowels in the spelling of old sources since they are almost never consistent on this point. Sometimes, when old sources contain *ar* the writer might have intended to represent a long *aa*, but it is just as possible that *a* plus following *r* or *rr* was meant.

Even with some writers who seem to have gone to a considerable amount of trouble to clearly mark long vowels, there can often be misleading spellings. For example, Gamilaraay words were written down by the missionary William Ridley in the 1860s in a fairly consistent spelling system. Ridley had studied a number of languages (including Latin and Greek) and lived in northern New South Wales for some time, getting a good grasp of the language. He uses a line over vowel sounds to show when they are long, as in 'guddū' for *guduu* 'cod fish' and 'karīl' for *garriil* 'cold'. Unfortunately, when the vowel follows the first letter of a word, Ridley's use of the line becomes inconsistent: sometimes the vowel is really long (as we know from later recordings), but sometimes it is short. Most Gamilaraay words have emphasis on the first vowel, and Ridley must have sometimes heard this as lengthening the vowel. For example, he writes 'būkhai' for *bagaay* 'creek', and 'mūrū' for *muru* 'nose'. Notice that he also slipped up in writing 'ar' where he should have had *ā* in 'pullar' for *balaa* 'white', and 'kārlin' for *gaalan* 'meat ant'.

Consonant sounds

Let us now look at consonant sounds. The examples that we have already looked at indicate that older spellings often vary in the following sorts of ways:

b	and	*p*	
d	and	*t*	
j	and	*ch*	(and also *g* before *i* or *e*)
g	and	*k*	(and also *c* or *ck*)

This is because it is common in Aboriginal languages for all the speakers of a language to pronounce words with sounds that are actually halfway between a *b* and a *p*, or between a *d* and a *t*. Sometimes, even if some people clearly pronounce a *g* or a *d*, other people might clearly pronounce the same words with *k* and *t*. Or the same person might pronounce a word with *b* on one occasion, but pronounce the same word with *p* on another occasion.

In languages where there are these kinds of variation (and you should remember that this covers most of the languages of Australia), you should settle on a single spelling for these sounds no matter what sorts of different spellings are given in the old sources. It does not matter whether you write all the words of the language with *p*'s, *t*'s and *k*'s (as is done in Pitjantjatjara), or with *b*'s, *d*'s and *g*'s (as is done in Bundjalung). The important thing is to write the sounds consistently in all the words that they are found in.

Another feature of Aboriginal languages is that they usually have more than one *r*-sound. One of these *r*-sounds is pronounced very much like the kind of 'softer' *r* we have in Australian English, while the other *r*-sound is rolled the way the Scots typically pronounce their *r*'s, or pronounced as a very quick flapping sound. Although the rolled *r* does not occur in the kind of English that is spoken in Australia, something very close to it is often found in words spelt with *t* or *d* between two vowels in words like 'butter' and 'ladder' when they are said quickly and casually.

The softer *r*-sound is often written in Aboriginal languages just as 'r', while the rolled *r* is often written double, as 'rr'. It is

important to indicate the difference between these two *r*-sounds
in Aboriginal languages, because the choice of one sound over
the other can often change the meaning of a word. For instance,
in the Gamilaraay language of north-central New South Wales,
we need to spell these two sounds differently to show the
difference between words such as the following:

> **muru**   nose
>
> **murru**   bottom, buttocks

(You wouldn't want to make a mistake if you were trying to
comment that somebody had a big nose, and you accidentally
ended up saying that they had an unusually large bottom!)

English speakers who wrote Aboriginal languages were often not
aware of the need to write these two sounds differently, so we
cannot always be certain about how sounds written as *r* should
be spelt. However, there are often clues in the kinds of spelling
variations that we find which tell us how words spelt with
r should be pronounced.

One clue involves variations between spellings with *r* and
spellings with *d*. If you find this kind of variation, you can be
reasonably sure that you are dealing with the rolled *r*, rather
than the softer *r*-sound. Bundjalung is one of those few
Australian languages which have only a single *r*-sound. Because
there is only one *r*-sound, we only need to use the single letter *r*,
though in its pronunciation, the Bundjalung *r* sounds just like
the *rr* that we find in other Aboriginal languages.

The word for 'bone' in this language was recorded by two different people as follows:

tarrigon

dadigun

The fact that one person has written 'rr', while the other has written 'd' suggests that the sound they were trying to represent was a rolled *r* rather than a *d*. We can confirm this guess by listening to the way that this word is pronounced by the old people today, who say *darigan*, and not 'dadigan'.

English speakers also seem to have had a lot of trouble writing words that end with the rolled *r*-sound. This is hard for English speakers to hear, firstly because we do not have rolled *r*'s in Australian English, and secondly because although we do have the softer *r*'s, we do not have them at the ends of words. (Although in Australia we do not pronounce *r*'s at the ends of words, they are pronounced by Americans, in words such as 'car' and 'four'.)

When these early observers tried to write Aboriginal words with a rolled *r* at the end, they often put in additional vowels instead, to make the words sound more like English words. So, if old sources have the same word ending sometimes in a vowel and sometimes *r*, the word may well have ended in a rolled *r*-sound. Sometimes when writers added a vowel at the end of a word, they also dropped the vowel that occurred before the *r*-sound.

Look at the following different ways that people wrote the
Bundjalung word for 'fire':

wybera

wibbera

wyborough

waibar

y-bur-a

wyebra

whyburra

The old Bundjalung people today pronounce this word as *waybar*,
and these early writers generally misheard this as 'waybra' or as
'waybara', and tried to spell it according to the pronunciation
that they had actually misheard. (Note that these spellings also
indicate that sometimes the old sources use letters of the
alphabet to stand for the sounds represented by the NAME of the
letter, and not just the sound that they represent. So, the
spelling 'y-bur-a' begins with the letter 'y', but we are supposed
to read this so that it sounds like the name of the letter itself).

Another thing that early writers often did when they heard
rolled *r*-sounds at the ends of words was to mishear them as
l-sounds, which are not really too different from *r*-sounds.
(Remember, for example, that Japanese people often have
trouble distinguishing *l*'s from *r*'s.) So, if you find variations in
spelling between *r* and *l* at the end of a word, it may be that you
are dealing with a rolled *r*.

Look at the following spellings of the word for 'one' in
Bundjalung:

yabbroo

yaburu

yabberu

yabul

The fact that there are vowels at the ends of words with the
letter *r* coming before them, and with the vowel before the
r being dropped should make you think that there is actually a
rolled *r* at the end of this word. That is, when early sources seem
to vary between spellings that point to pronunciations such as
'yabru' and 'yaburu', they were probably trying to represent
something more like *yabur*.

You can see that the last of these spellings is actually closest to
this suggested pronunciation, except that the writer has
incorrectly written the final sound as *l*. When you see these
kinds of variations in spellings, you should also be suspicious
that the last sound was meant to be a rolled *r*. Once again, we
can confirm this guess by checking with the old people, who
pronounce the word for 'one' in Bundjalung as *yabur*.

In English, the letters *th* are used to represent two different
sounds. Firstly, they can represent the sound in the word 'this',
and secondly, they can represent the sound in 'thin'. Neither of
these sounds occurs in most Aboriginal languages. However,
there is another sound that occurs in many Aboriginal

languages that is not found in English. This is a sound that is halfway between sounds that we write as *d* or *t*, and the sounds that we write as *th*, sounding very much like the sounds in 'go**t the**' and 'ha**d the**'. In many Aboriginal languages, this sound is written as *dh*, or as *th*.

For instance, in the Gamilaraay language of north-central New South Wales, there are words such as the following, where it is important to distinguish between words spelt with *d* and words spelt with *th* (as well as words spelt with *dj*) because there is very often little else that distinguishes between these words. Look at the following examples:

madamada	knotty (as hair)
matha	women's marriage division
madja	exclamation of sorrow

Although some writers misheard this sound as *th*, there are plenty of other writers who couldn't hear it as a separate sound at all, and simply represented it as *t* or *d*. This means that if you come across examples of variation in spelling between *t* and *d* and *th*, then the sound that you are dealing with could well be *th*.

There are other writers who also found the sound that we spell in Aboriginal languages as *dj* or *tj* (or sometimes as *dy* and *ty*) difficult to distinguish from the sounds that we spell as *d* or *t*. Where you find variation in spellings between *ch* or *j* (or *dge* at the ends of words) and *t* or *d*, it may well be that you are dealing with the sound *dj*.

Languages spoken in central and western Australia have a further type of *d*-sound, one in which the tongue tip is turned back slightly (we call these retroflex sounds, something like the pronunciation of a person from India or Pakistan). We write this sound as *rd*. English speakers have trouble with this sound, but we can sometimes tell it is present when the spelling contains a vowel (usually *e, u* or *o*) plus *rt* or *rd*, as in the following examples from Diyari, spoken east of Lake Eyre:

Wordlist spelling	Correct spelling	English meaning
murtie	**mardi**	heavy
wordoo	**wardu**	short
merda	**marda**	stone

Aboriginal languages don't often have words starting with vowel sounds. If you see words written in old sources that start with vowels, you should be suspicious that maybe they contain some kind of mistake, and that the European writer was actually mishearing a vowel for something else. Aboriginal languages do not usually have words containing *h*-sounds either, so you should also be suspicious of words in old sources with the letter *h*, especially if it comes at the beginnings of words.

One thing that Aboriginal languages do have, which English does not have, are words starting with the sound *ng*. English words do have this sound, but only in the middle of words (such as 'singer'), or at the end of words (as in 'bang'). The sound *ng* at the beginning of words in Aboriginal languages is very hard for English speakers to hear. Sometimes they would not hear this sound at all. Sometimes they would hear it, but they would mistake it for an *n* or *m*, or for an *h*, or for a *g*. So, when you see the same word starting with spellings that vary between *h*, *g*, *m* or *n*, or which sometimes have just a vowel at the beginning, there is a good chance it starts with the *ng*-sound.

Look at the following spellings of the Bundjalung word for 'dog':

augham

aggum

nuccum

nargum

We would expect that this would should have *ng* at the beginning. The next sound would be *a*. With the variation between spellings such as *g* and *c*, we can be sure that the next sound should be *g*. The final part of the word should be *am*. Thus, we would guess that the word should be *ngagam*, and this is exactly what the old Bundjalung people tell us it should be.

Aboriginal languages often have an *n*-sound like in English 'onion' or 'news'. In many Aboriginal languages, this sound is written as *ny* (though sometimes, it is spelt instead as *yn* at the ends of words). English only has this *ny*-sound at the beginning and in the middle of words, but it never has the *ny*-sound at the end of words. This makes it very difficult for English speakers to hear when it occurs at the ends of words.

Typically, when English speakers come across the *ny*-sound at the end of a word, they mishear it as *n*, or as *ng*. These are both sounds that do occur at the end of words in English, so it is easy for English speakers to hear them. When there is a *ny* at the end of a word in an Aboriginal language, this may also cause an English speaker to mishear the vowel that comes before it as an *i*-sound as well, or for there to be a *y*-sound between the vowel and the final consonant (giving spellings like *ain* or *oin*). So, if you find spellings that vary between *n* and *ng*, especially when there seems to be inconsistency in the spelling of the vowels before these sounds as well, it may be that there should be a *ny*-sound at the end of the word.

Look at the following early spellings of the Bundjalung word for 'tongue':

yalling

yullan

We can be fairly certain that the first part of this word should be written as *yal*-. The variation between the *i* and *a* spellings, as well as the variation between the *ng* and *n* spellings, suggests that it should probably be correctly spelt as *yalayn*. (Remember that the letters *yn* at the end of a word in Bundjalung spell the same sound that is written as *ny* at the beginning and in the middle of words such as *nyula* 'he' and *ganyahl* 'fishing line'.)

It is possible to imagine a number of other spellings that early writers might have given for a word pronounced *yalayn* in an

Aboriginal language. Other possible spellings pointing to the same pronunciation might include the following:

yullain

yallane

yalline

yullin

yaline

yalyne

yaling

Although English does have *ny*-sounds at the beginning and in the middle of words (in words like 'news' and 'banyan'), these do not sound exactly like the sounds that are written as *ny* in Aboriginal languages. This is because the *ny*-sounds in English really consist of an ordinary *n*-sound with a following *y*-sound. However, in Aboriginal languages, the sound that is written as *ny* is really just a single sound, which is halfway between *n* and *y* in its pronunciation .

This means that what should be correctly written in Aboriginal languages as *ny* is often misheard as just *n* or *y*. Where you see spellings that vary between *n* and *y*, there is a good chance that the writer was mishearing this *ny*-sound.

Although English speakers sometimes had trouble writing *ng*-sounds and *ny*-sounds in some parts of words, there are some other sounds that they almost always had trouble writing. In fact, many writers never heard these sounds at all, which means that for many words in some languages, we can never be completely sure whether our spellings are correct or not.

Some languages have a sound that is more or less halfway between the *th*-sound and the *ny*-sound. In those languages that have this sound, it is often written as *nh*. In Yuwaaliyaay of north-central New South Wales, it is important to write this sound differently to both *n* and *ny* as sometimes this is just about all that is used to distinguish different words from each other. Look at the following words:

guna   shit

gunharr   kangaroo rat

To an English speaker, these words would sound almost identical, yet a speaker of Yuwaaliyaay would hear the difference without any trouble. No doubt you can appreciate how important it would be to clearly distinguish the pronunciation (and spelling) of these two words in this language. Imagine the consequences of any possible mistakes!

Similarly, in central and western Australian languages there is an *n*-sound pronounced with the tongue tip turned backwards (like *rd* we described above). We write this as *rn*, but in the early sources it sometimes appears as 'rn' and sometimes just as 'n'. Examples from Diyari are 'merna' for *marna* 'mouth', and 'achana' for *ngadjarna* 'to ask'.

The problem is that in nearly all of the earlier sources, words containing the *nh* or *rn*-sound would have been written with the letter *n*, which also represents the *n*-sound. This means that if your language is one of those which has separate *nh* or *rn*-sounds and you see a spelling such as 'noodil', you can never be sure whether the first letter is meant to represent *n* or *nh* or *rn*. So, a spelling like this could be interpreted just as easily as being meant to represent 'nudil' or 'rnudil' (or 'ngudil') as 'nhudil'.

In fact, if you only have a single spelling for this word, there are some other pronunciations that you could not rule out as well. An early spelling such as 'noodil' could therefore easily also have been meant to represent any one of the following kinds of pronunciation:

nudil	**nuthil**	**nudjil**	**nurdil**
nhudil	**nhuthil**	**nhudjil**	**nhurdil**
nyudil	**nyuthil**	**nyudjil**	**nyurdil**
ngudil	**nguthil**	**ngudjil**	**ngurdil**
rnudil	**rnuthil**	**rnudjil**	**rnurdil**

In cases like this, we can only decide which of this whole range of possibilities is correct by asking one of the old people what the correct pronunciation of the word is. Unfortunately, if it happens that there are no old people left who still remember the word, we can never be certain about which pronunciation was correct.

This kind of ambiguity can also come about when consonants come together in the middle of a word. Thus, a spelling like *ng* in the middle of a word could indicate:

- the single sound *ng*, as in 'singer';

■   the sequences of sounds *n* followed by *g* (we write this
    as *n.g*), as in mankind;

■   *ng* followed by *g* (*ngg*), as in finger;

■   *n* followed by *dj* (*ndj*), as in whinger.

For example, 'cangell' for *ganggal*, or 'carnungool' for *ganundjul*.

Aboriginal languages rarely have the kinds of rasping 'noisy'
sounds that we write as *s, sh, z, f* and *v* in English. You should be
suspicious of any words in an early source that contain these
letters. It could be that these letters represent printing mistakes,
but it is also possible that these sounds represent a sound that
somebody misheard. The sounds that these letters are most
likely to represent are as follows:

s, sh, z	represent	*tj, dj* (also spelt as *ty* or *dy*)
f, v	represent	*p, b*

Using these kinds of general guiding principles it is often
possible to compare spellings to one another and to arrive at a
reasonable idea of how the word should be pronounced.

Printing mistakes

If we did not have enough problems already in correctly
interpreting old spellings, there is the final problem
that old published sources often include mistakes that the
writers did not discover when their material was published. If it
is at all possible, you should check the spelling of a doubtful
form against the spelling in the original handwritten

manuscripts. Some of the more common printing errors that you
will expect to find are interchanges of the following letters:

u	and	*n*
n	and	*m*
n	and	*r*
l	and	*t*
i	and	*j*
i	and	*l*
g	and	*y*

There may also be confusion between *o, a, e* and *s*, because in
the handwriting of the time, it was often difficult to decide
exactly which letter people were intending to write (especially if
the ink has faded over the years). See Jaki Troy's chapter (p 37)
for more discussion of interpreting old handwriting.

For instance, there is a whole variety of different sources which
indicate that the word in Bundjalung for 'hand' should be
written as *danggan*. However, there is just one old source which
gives the word as 'tungau'. This spelling by itself would probably
be more consistent with a number of other pronunciations,
including 'danggaw' or 'dangga' or 'danggu', but certainly not
danggan. Probably what happened is that in this single source,
somebody mistakenly printed the *n* upside down, and it came
out as a *u*! This means that it was meant to have been printed as
'tungan', and not as 'tungau' at all.

Using information from other languages

ometimes the source information that we have on a particular language is quite poor in quality, or limited in scope, and we are unable to decide which is the correct pronunciation of a word from among a number of possibilities. Occasionally, we can look at information on neighbouring languages and use that to help us decide. We have to be careful when comparing neighbouring languages to realise that sometimes their words will be different, but on many occasions there will be enough similarities that these can help us decide between a number of competing alternatives.

For example, the Gamilaraay language of north-central New South Wales ceased to be spoken in the 1950s as a result of the policies of the New South Wales government that prevented older people passing on their knowledge to younger generations. We have a little information on the language from professional records made in 1955 by S.A. Wurm, and lots of early recordings collected by missionaries and settlers. The language which was the western neighbour of Gamilaraay is called Yuwaaliyaay — it continued to be spoken until the 1980s and we have good records of it, including tape recordings. We can use this information to compare with Gamilaraay old sources to help sort out spellings.

In general, Gamilaraay words and Yuwaaliyaay words look pretty similar. Where there are differences between a pair of words in the two languages, we often find that the same kind of difference is found in many other words at the same time. For instance, when Gamilaraay has the soft *r*-sound between identical vowels, Yuwaaliyaay has no *r* and just a long vowel. Here are some examples:

Gamilaraay	Yuwaaliyaay	English meaning
mara	maa	hand
biri	bii	chest
yuru	yuu	cloud, dust

There are lots more examples of this type of difference in words in the two languages. However, when there is a rolled *r* between two identical vowels in Gamilaraay, we do not find any difference at all between the two languages. This means that Gamilaraay *rr* corresponds to Yuwaaliyaay *rr*, as in the following words, which are the same in both languages:

Gamilaraay	Yuwaaliyaay	English meaning
barra	barra	to fly
mirril	mirril	nasal mucus, snot
burrul	burrul	big
murrun	murrun	alive

Now, we can use this comparative information on the two languages to help in interpreting some of the spellings in old Gamilaraay sources. First, look at the following spellings for the word for 'black swan':

barriamul	pariamul
parrearmel	parrimul

We can line these spellings up and use the principles we described earlier to work out the correct spelling:

b	a	rr	ia	m	u	l
p	a	r	ia	m	u	l
p	a	rr	ear	m	e	l
p	a	rr	i	m	u	l
b	**a**	**??**	**aya**	**m**	**a**	**l**

The problem is: what about the sound that is written alternately as *r* and *rr*? These spellings could equally well have been meant to represent 'barayamal' or 'barrayamal'.

Looking at Yuwaaliyaay, we find that its word for 'black swan' is *baayamal*. This fits with the kinds of correspondences between the two languages where there is a soft *r*-sound between the two vowels, so we can guess that the original sound was probably *r* and not *rr*. The reconstituted spelling for 'black swan' in Gamilaraay should therefore be *barayamal*.

Now look at this example of the spellings for 'black duck' in Gamilaraay:

kurranghi

yurrungee

currunga

koorangee

kurrongey

koorangee

We can line these up as follows:

k	u	rr	a	n	gh	i
y	u	rr	u	n	g	ee
c	u	rr	u	n	g	a
k	oo	r	a	n	g	ee
k	u	rr	o	n	g	ey
k	oo	r	a	n	g	ee
g	a	??	a	??	g	??

Here we have several problems:

- What is the *r*-sound?

- What is the final sound?

- Was the sound before the *g* really an *n*, or could it have been the *ng*-sound?

On the basis of the spellings in the Gamilaraay sources, the final sound could have been *i* (suggested by 'ee') or *ay* (suggested by 'ey', and the letter names *a* and *i*). The *r*-sound could have been *r* or *rr*. Thus, any of the following would be pronunciations that these spellings could have been trying to represent:

garangay	**garanggay**
garrangay	**garranggay**
garangi	**garanggi**
garrangi	**garranggi**

In Yuwaaliyaay, the word 'black duck' has been correctly recorded as *garrangay*. Since this is one of the possible pronunciations that is consistent with the various Gamilaraay sources, we should assume that this was probably the original form of the Gamilaraay word as well.

While information from neighbouring languages can help us out in cases like this, we should point out that it is very easy to misuse information from other languages, especially if you are not trained in how languages change over time, and how languages are related to each other. If you are thinking that perhaps this kind of information might be able to help you to interpret some sources for a particular language, it would probably be best to ask for help from an experienced linguist. ■

Exercise 1

The word for 'fly' in Gamilaraay appears in old sources as:

burulu

budulu

boorooloo

poodeloo

buriloo

What do you think the correct spelling should be?

Answer

The different spellings of **p** and **b** at the beginning of the word show variants of a sound **b**. The use of **u** and **oo** for the next sound suggests **u**. The next sound is spelled as **r** or **d** and we saw that this indicated the rolled **r**, rather than the smooth r-sound. The next sound is also **u**, as indicated by **u** and **oo** (in Gamilaraay main emphasis generally goes on the first syllable, so middle vowels tend to sound weaker and more indistinct to English speakers. This is why we also get **e** and **i** in the spellings here). The next sound is invariably **l**, while the final sound is again **u**.

This gives us: **burrulu**. Wurm's notes from 1955 confirm this as the correct pronunciation. ■

Exercise 2

The word for 'bone' in Bundjalung is spelt in old sources as:

tarregun   **derigun**   **duregan**

tarrigon   **dadigun**

What do you think the correct spelling should be?

Answer

The variation between the spellings **t** and **d** at the beginning of the word indicates that the difference between these sounds is not important, as we find in very many Aboriginal languages. We should settle on only one of these to write all examples of such variation, and in the case of the accepted Bundjalung spelling, the choice has been to spell these sounds as **d**. The **a** spellings, as well as the **u** and **e** spellings, all point to the next sound being an **a**. There is only one **r**-sound in Bundjalung (though in most Aboriginal languages there are two separate **r**-sounds, a 'softer' sound which is generally written as **r**, and a 'stronger' sound that is generally written double, as **rr**). This means that we only need to write this as **r** in Bundjalung. The fact that one of these spellings contains a **d** is because the **r**-sound in Bundjalung is in fact pronounced rather more 'strongly' than the normal **r** of English. This caused the person writing this word to hear it as the same kind of sound that we sometimes make in English when we pronounce a word like 'steady' very casually. The variation between the spellings **a**, **o** and **u** all point to the sound being **a**. Finally, the last sound is consistently spelt as **n**, so there are no problems in deciding that it should be spelt as **n**.

The correct spelling of this word in Bundjalung should be **darigan**. ■

Exercise 3

The word for 'wood' in one of the Tasmanian Aboriginal languages was spelt as follows by English people:

moo.mer.rer   **mume.mer.rer**

moomerah   **moomara**

The same word was recorded by French people as follows:

moumra   **moumbra**

What do you think the correct spelling should be?

Answer

The first part of this word was almost certainly **mu**. The spellings **oo** in English and **ou** in French both suggest that the second sound was **u**. Other spellings such as **mume** in English for this part of the word also suggest that the second sound was **u**. All sources point to the next sound being another **m**. All sources also point to the last sound being **a**. There are a few problems with the middle of the word, however. The English sources suggest that following the second **m**-sound, there was a vowel, which is spelt as either **a** or **e**. In the French sources, however, there is no vowel at all. This could be interpreted as meaning two different things:

- There really was a vowel there, but the first vowel may have been more strongly emphasised, leaving the vowel in the middle of the word 'swallowed up' a little bit, making it harder to hear for the French people. If there was a vowel here, then it was probably **a**, given that there is variation between the spellings **a** and **e**. *continued...*

- There was no vowel here at all, and the English speakers put one in where it shouldn't have been, in much the same way that some people speaking English say 'fillum' instead of 'film', or 'burgular' instead of 'burglar'.

We also have to decide how to represent the r-sounds. You will notice that one of the French recorders has written a b between the m and the r. This might have been because the sound that he wrote as r was pronounced very strongly. In olden times in English, our r-sounds were pronounced much more strongly than they are nowadays (more like the Scots roll their r's today).

When our rolled r's came after sounds like n, people sometimes inserted a d-sound between the n and the r. There was once a word 'thunrian' in English, which people came to pronounce as 'thundrian'. This has come down to us today as the word 'thunder', but the d in that word was originally not there at all.

What could have happened in the case of the spelling moumbra by the French writer is that he was hearing something like mumarra (or mumrra), but because there was a rolled r-sound, he might have inserted the b when it should not really have been there, in the same way that English speakers in the past once put the d in the word 'thunder'.

So, in the case of the word for 'wood' in this Tasmanian language, we cannot be sure from the written records whether these spellings were meant to represent the pronunciation mumarra, or mumrra. This is one of the few words of Tasmanian languages that have been remembered down to modern times, and one of the grand-daughters of one of the women who was born in the Flinders Island settlement in the 1800s was recorded on tape with a pronunciation something like **mumara**. She pronounced a vowel after the second **m**, but her **r**-sound was very soft, like the normal Australian English **r**, and not rolled like the Scots **r**. However, we cannot take this old lady's pronunciation as necessarily meaning that the original pronunciation had a soft **r**, as people who speak only English often find it quite difficult to pronounce rolled **r**'s.

What all of this means is that the original pronunciation of the word for 'wood' was probably **mumarra**, though we cannot rule out other possibilities, such as **mumara**, or **mumrra**, or even **mumra**. ■

Exercise 4

Look at the following spellings of the Gamilaraay word for 'right hand':

> **thurial**
>
> **toorial**
>
> **turial**
>
> **tooreal**

What do you think the correct spelling should be? (Hint: 'right hand' in Yuwaaliyaay is **thuuyaal**).

Answer

The **t** and **th** at the beginning here indicate **th**. The next sound is **u**, as shown by spellings **u** and **oo**. Next we have an **r**, but we cannot tell if it represents **r** or **rr**. The next sequence of **ia** or **ea** probably represents something like **iya** or **uya**, while the ending is clearly **l**. On the basis of the old sources we would say the word is **thur(r?)i/uyal**. Now, when we look at Yuwaaliyaay we find **thuu** at the beginning; this points to Gamilaraay having **thuru** (remember that when Gamilaraay has **r** between identical vowels, Yuwaaliyaay just has two vowels and this helps us decide between **r** and **rr**). As for the ending, the old writers of Gamilaraay probably missed the long vowel **aa**, so we can use the comparative information from Yuwaaliyaay to say that the Gamilaraay word for 'right hand' was probably **thuruyaal**. ∎

Exercise 5

The word for 'ear' in a Tasmanian Aboriginal language is spelt in the
following ways by the same person, writing on different occasions:

> **nin.ne.woon.er**
>
> **hen.ne.wun.ner**
>
> **un.ne.woo.ner**

What do you think the correct spelling of this word should be?

Answer

The hardest part of this word is probably the beginning, so we will
leave that till last. The spellings **woon** and **wun** probably point to a
pronunciation like **wun**. (It is significant to note that the Englishman
who wrote these words was a poorly educated lower class man,
who spoke a dialect of English where the word **but** rhymes with
put.) The last sound was probably meant to be **a**. Thus, the word
probably ended in **wuna**. If we assume that Tasmanian had only
three vowels — **i**, **u** and **a** — then the **e** that precedes the **w** is a
problem. In order to work out whether this should be **i** or **a** (as
both are possible), then we really need some more spellings which
point in the correct direction. However, we simply do not have any
more spellings, so we cannot decide between these two alternatives.
The next preceding sound is fairly straightforward, as it was almost
certainly **n**. The vowel that comes before this is our biggest
headache in deciding the correct spelling of this word. The spelling **i**
suggests that it was **i**, whereas the spelling **u** suggests that it was
either **u** or **a**. The spelling **e** could be interpreted as either **i** or **a**.

continued...

This spelling is therefore completely ambiguous between all three vowels, and there is no way that we can decide which is correct!

The first sound of the word might look like a problem as well, though perhaps it is not as big a problem as it first seems. Variations in spelling between **n**, **h** and nothing often points to the sound **ng** that English speakers often have so much trouble with at the beginning of a word.

So, what we have is a set of spellings that point in any of the following directions:

nginiwuna	**nganiwuna**	**nguniwuna**
nginawuna	**nganawuna**	**ngunawuna**

Unfortunately, in this case, there is no longer anybody left who remembers enough of the language to be able to help us decide which of these possibilities is correct. ■

inguists working on Australian Aboriginal languages
have not written much about the problems of working
out spellings from old sources, so really there is nothing you can
read that will give you more details on these kinds of problems
apart from what we have said. However, there are a couple of
books and articles that mention some of the problems that we
have described, and use the techniques we have discussed. You
may wish to look at them for further ideas.

Austin, Peter 1991, The Karangura Language, *Records of the South
Australian Museum* 25, 129–37.

Blake, Barry J 1991, Woiwurrung, the Melbourne Language. In RMW
Dixon and Barry J Blake (eds), *The Handbook of Australian
Languages*, vol 4, 30–122. Melbourne: Oxford University Press
[especially pages 58–62].

Breen, Gavan 1981, *The Mayi Languages of the Queensland Gulf
Country*. Canberra: Australian Institute of Aboriginal and
Torres Strait Islander Studies.

Breen, Gavan 1990, Salvage Studies of Western Queensland Aboriginal
Languages. Canberra: *Pacific Linguistics*.

Crowley, Terry and RMW Dixon 1981, Tasmanian. In RMW Dixon and
Barry J Blake (eds), *Handbook of Australian Languages*, vol 2,
394–421 [especially pages 404–414]. Canberra: Australian
National University Press.

Hercus, Luise 1989, Three Linguistic Studies from Southwestern New
South Wales, *Aboriginal History* 13, 44–62.

Oates, Lynette 1990, Aboriginal Recording of Aboriginal Language. In Peter Austin, RMW Dixon, Tom Dutton and Isobel White (eds), Language and History: Essays in Honour of Luise Hercus, 221–232. Canberra: *Pacific Linguistics*, C–116.

Ganai—a lost opprotunity

In 1963, Luise Hercus recorded several speakers of Ganai (a Gippsland language) including Jack Connolly of Fitzroy. Jack, then in his seventies, recalled some language from his early days at Lake Tyers and words he had learnt from his mother. Jack's mother was born at Yarram and spoke all the Ganai dialects fluently. She cherished her knowledge and before her death in the 1940s, at the urging of a local pastor, wrote down an entire vocabulary of her Yarram dialect. When Luise Hercus met Jack Connolly in 1963 only one page remained, the rest having been destroyed by children who did not realise its importance. ■

Nicholas Thieberger

How to decide on a spelling system

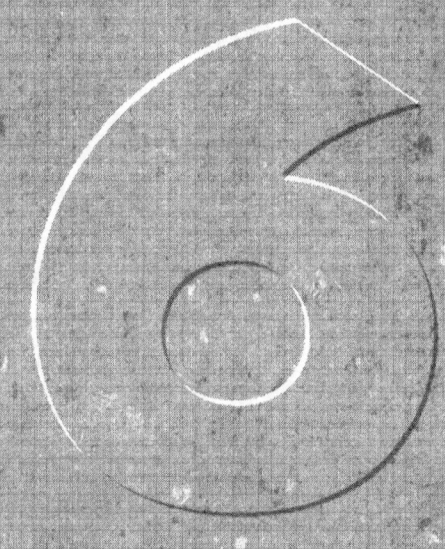

How to decide on a spelling system

In other parts of this book we have seen that untrained people recording Australian languages often made mistakes because they tried to use the spelling system of their own language. Each language has its own system of sounds, and it is by finding out what those sounds are and how they work in the language that we can then develop a good spelling system. Ideally a spelling system should aim to show what the meaningful sounds of a language are.

Can't we use the English system?

English has a spelling system that got stuck a few hundred years ago and has not been able to keep up with changes in the language. It has also had words from other languages coming in at various times and on top of all of that, scholars changed the spelling system to try and show the origins of words, so we got stuck with a *b* in debt, *p* in receipt and *h* in honour. The spelling we use in English does its best and really does very well, but it also has lots of ways of spelling the same sounds. Think about words like these in which the bolded parts are all the same sounds:

eye	**aye**	wh**y**	s**igh**	p**i**	p**ie**	**I**
c**ow**	b**ough**					
k**i**t	wom**e**n					
s**ew**	h**oe**	cr**ow**	pr**o**	th**ough**		

Now think of examples which use the same spelling, but are pronounced differently:

b**ough**	c**ough**	thr**ough**
h**ow**	t**ow**	

The problem of trying to write an Australian indigenous language using an English spelling system has been the topic of other parts of this book. When we come to design a spelling system for a language that has not been written before, we can make it much more sensible than the English one.

We should try to make the spelling system so that one sound in the language has one letter. All spelling systems which linguists help develop should follow this approach, each sound having one symbol. There are good spelling systems in use all over Australia, used in schools, in major reference works like dictionaries and in other books. The chart on pages 112–113 shows some variant spellings that have been used in the past and compares them with the spelling systems of some of the languages mentioned in this book.

In the next few pages you will see examples of spelling systems from different languages. Sometimes neighbouring languages can use the same spelling system, so if you know the sound system of a nearby language, and it is similar to the one you are working on (they could be related languages like Italian, French and Spanish) then you may be able to use the same spelling system (see the discussion in Chapter 5 on using information from other languages).

However, you have to be careful. Warlpiri, Arrernte and Pitjantjatjara are geographically close to each other, but each has a different sound system and uses a different spelling system.

The following charts (pages 106–11) are given to show what systems are being used and what you can expect to find in your area. The maps give a general location of the country of the language; they are not meant to show what the boundaries of the language group are. (They show the 1:1,000,000 map on which the country associated with the language occurs.)

Note that there are many similarities among the sound systems of Australian languages, and so the spelling systems are also often similar or identical.

Adnyamathanha (Yura Ngawarla)

	labial	inter-dental	alveolar	retroflex	lamino palatal	velar
stop	p	th	t	rt	ty	k
voiced stop	b	dh	d	rd	dy	
fricative	vnh					
nasal	m	lh	n	rn	ny	ng
lateral			l	rl	ly	
flap			d	rd		
trill			rr			
glide	w		r		y	

vowels   a aa i u

Arrente (Eastern Arrente)

	labial	inter-dental	alveolar	retroflex	lamino-palatal	velar
stop	p	th	t	rt	ty	k
nasal	m	nh	n	rn	ny	ng
pre-stopped	pm	tnh	tn	rtn	tny	kng
lateral		lh	l	rl	ly	
trill		rr				
glide	w	r	y		h	

vowels   a e i u

Burarra - Gun-nartpa

	bilabial	alveolar	retroflex	lamino-palatal	velar
stop	p	t	rt	ch	k
voiced stop	b	d	rd	j	g
nasal	m	n	rn	ny	ng
lateral		l	rl	ly	
flap, trill		rr	rd		
glide	w		r	y	

vowels   a e i o u

Gupapuyŋu

	bilabial	dental	alveolar	retroflex	lamino-palatal	velar	glottal
stop	p/b	th/dh	t/d	ṯ/ḏ	tj/dj	k/g	'
nasal	m	nh	n	ṉ	ny	ŋ	
lateral			l	ḻ			
flap, trill			rr				
glide	w			r	y		

vowels   a ä e i o u

Gurindji

	bilabial	alveolar	retroflex	lamino palatal	velar
stop	p	t	rt	j	k
nasal	m	n	rn	ny	ng
lateral		l	rl	ly	
flap, trill		rr			
glide	w		r	y	

vowels   a i u

Jaru

	bilabial	alveolar	retroflex	lamino-palatal	velar
stop	b	d	rd	j	g
nasal	m	n	rn	ny	ng
lateral	l	rl	ly		
flap, trill	rr	rd			
glide	w	r	y		

vowels	a aa i ii u uu

Ngarluma

	bilabial	dental	alveolar	retroflex	lamino-palatal	velar
stop	b	th	d	rd	j	k/g
nasal	m	nh	n	rn	ny	ng
lateral		lh	l	rl ‘	ly	
flap, trill			rr	rd		
glide	w			r	y	

vowels	a i u

Paakantyi

	bilabial	dental	alveolar	retroflex	lamino-palatal	velar
stop	p	th	t	rd	ty	k
nasal	m	nh	n	rn	ny	ng
lateral		lh	l	rl	ly	
flap, trill			rr	rd		
glide	w			r	y	

vowels   a aa i ii u uu

Pitjantjatjara

	bilabial	alveolar	retroflex	lamino-palatal	velar
stop	p	t	t̠	tj	k
nasal	m	n	n̠	ny	ng
lateral		l	l̠	ly	
flap, trill		r			
glide	w		r̠	y	

vowels   a a: i i: u u:

Wik-Mungkan

	bilabial	dental	alveolar	retroflex	lamino-palatal	velar	glottal
stop	p	th	t		ch	k	'
nasal	m	nh	n		ny	ng	
lateral			l				
flap, trill			rr				
glide	w			r	y		

vowels	a aa e ee i ii o oo u uu	

he following table lists letters and other symbols that have been used in historical sources together with descriptions of the sounds they have been used to represent. As pointed out elsewhere in this book, it is important to know where a writer comes from, and to understand the effect of their own language's spelling system on their choice of symbols.

Letters, sounds and how to say them

The column 'Most common spelling' shows the set of letters and pairs of letters most commonly drawn on in modern spelling systems for writing Australian languages. There are no phonetic characters or diacritics, which makes them easy to use with computers.

The table is based on Yallop (1982) with three extra columns for the spelling systems of the languages mentioned most often in this book, so you have a key for reading Bundjalung, Gamilaraay and Kaurna words aloud.

Most common spelling	Bundjalung spelling	Gamilaraay spelling	Kaurna spelling	Similar English sound
a	a	a	a	as in about, cut
aa	ah	aa		as in father
b / p	b	b	b /p	between English b and p
d / t	d	d	d / t	between English t and d
dh / th	dh	th		made with your tongue blade pressed against the back of your top front teeth, as for a th sound in English
	e	eh		
e	eh			sometimes used as a long i sound, otherwise like e in her
g	g	g	g / k	between English k and g, occasionally written as k when at the beginning of a word
i	i	i	i / e	as in pin
ii	ih	ii		as in peel
j	j	dj	ty	sometimes like j in budge, sometimes like ch in catcher
l	l	l	l	like English l
lh				made by saying l with your tongue blade pressed against the back of your top front teeth
ly			ly	as in million
m	m	m	m	like English m
n	n	n	n	like English n
ng	ŋ	ng	ng	like ng in singer
nh		nh		made by saying n with your tongue blade pressed against the back of your top front teeth
ny	ny/ yn	ny	ny	as in onion
'				glottal stop, like in cockney pronunciation of tt in bottle
r	r	r	rr	like r in English run, with the tongue tip turned back
rd / rt			rt	like t said with the tongue tip curled backwards
rl			rl	like l said with the tongue tip curled backwards
rn			rn	like n said with the tongue tip curled backwards
rr		rr	r / rr	a trilled r like in Italian or Scottish English
u	u	u	u / o	as in put
uu	uh	uu		as in cool
w	w	w	w	like English w
y	y	y	y	like English y

Phonetic symbol	Linguistic description	Other letters and symbols that have often been used
a	low back vowel	a, ah, ar, o, u
aː	long low back vowel	a, ah, ar
b / p	bilabial stop	
d	alveolar stop	t
	interdental stop	dh, th, ḍ, ṭ
e / ɛ / iː	long high front vowel	i
g	velar stop	c, cc, k
i	high front vowel	e, ee, y
iː	long high front vowel	e, ee, y, iy, ih
dʒ / tʃ	alveolar affricate	c, ch, dy, dy, dj, tj, ty, ty
l	alveolar lateral	
ḻ	interdental lateral	l
λ	palatal lateral	l, gl, lj, ly
m	bilabial nasal	
n	alveolar nasal	
ŋ	velar nasal	gn, n, ŋ
ṉ	interdental nasal	n, ṉ
ɲ	palatal nasal	gn, nj, ny, ñ
ʔ	glottal stop	h
ɹ	retroflex glide or approximant	R, r, ɽ
ɭ	retroflex stop	d,t, d, t, ṭ, ḍ
ḷ / ɭ	retroflex lateral	l
ɳ / ṇ	retroflex nasal	n, ṇ
r / ɾ	alveolar flap or trill	r, d, ř
u / ʊ	high back unrounded vowel	o, oo
uː	long high back unrounded vowel	o, oo
w	labiovelar or bilabial glide	
j	palatal glide	j, i

Workshop exercises

Exercise 1 — Sound systems

These exercises aim to show how sound systems work and how they are or are not reflected by spelling systems.

1 Circle the following pairs of words which differ in only one sound.

pig / big   cat / dog   pit / bit

does / goes   in / it   fat / thin

heart / cart   hate / wait

2 Circle the silent letters in the following words:

kneel   talk   comb   sign   island   honest

3 Circle the parts of the following pairs that have the same sound. Notice that the same sound can be represented by different letters.

enough / full   women / trip

knight / plan   loose / snooze

which / catch   thing / breathing

4 What do these exercises tell us about the spelling system of English?

5 Write the following words using a practical spelling system.

a. Gundagai   b. Woolloomooolloo

c. Kununurra   d. Pardoo

e. Mia Mia   f. Coolgardie ■

Exercise 2 — Spelling

Look through either a dictionary or a wordlist of an Australian
language. Find a word that contains the following sound and write it
in the space provided. Practise pronouncing the words as you read
them and copy them.

a

i

j

k

l

lh

ly

m

n

ng

nh

ny

p

r

rl

rn

rr

rt

t

th

u

w

y

Exercise 3

Look at this example text in Manjiljarra, a language of the Great Sandy Desert. Written by Mitchell Biljaba.

Ngayu-rna yutirringu Nyika-ngka Taakuruutu-ngka nyarra-karti.
I was born over past the Stock Route at Nyika.

Nyika-ngka kakarra Jilukurru-ngka.
Nyika is east of Durba Hills.

Maa-rni-ya kanyirnu yuwinmanu.
My family kept me and "grew me up".

Palunyajanu-rni-ya katingu kakarra Yirnangarri.
After that they took me east to Yirnangarri

Payarr-wana Puyulykura-wana.
around Payarr and around Puyulykura.

Puyulykura-ngka-ya nyinangu pakarnu Maliki...Jukurrpa.
At Puyulykura Maliki people stayed and then got up...in the Dreamtime.

Ka-ya yanu kakarra.
And they went to the east.

Ka-laju yanu marlaku Taakuruutu-karti.
And we went back to the Stock Route.

Jiingulyu-laju nyinangu rawa.
We stayed there a long time.

Maa-rna kuka pungurringu.
I learned how to kill animals (for meat).

Palunyajanu-lajura yanu Mamurnarra-karti.
After that we went on to Mamurnarra.

continued...

Ka-laju-jananya watijunu jina pulukuwinti yanunyja.

> *And we followed the tracks of the people taking the cattle [on the Stock Route].*

Pungu-ya ngalangu junu tarrka puluku.

> *They killed and ate a bullock and left the bones.*

Ka-laju manu paarnu ngalangu.

> *And we got [what was left] and cooked it and ate it.*

Ka-laju yanu yapurra Karlamilyi-karti.

> *And we went west to Rudall River.*

Fill in the English words for the following (1 and 2 are done for you).

1	**-laju**	we
2	**-wana**	around
3	**-rna**	
4	**Ka**	
5	**yapurra**	
6	**puluku**	
7	**-ya**	
8	**ngalangu**	
9	**yanu**	
10	**-ngka**	
11	**kakarra**	
12	**-ku**	
13	**-karti**	
14	**-rni**	
15	**marlaku**	
16	**Taakuruutu**	

Exercise 4 — Ngarluma language

Look carefully at these sentences from Ngarluma, one of the languages of the area around Roebourne.

1 Ngayi   nyinku   nhaku-ru   birri-ngka
   I (subject)   you (object)   see (-future)   afternoon (-place)

   I'll see you in the afternoon

2 Balu   ngaju   thalku-nha   warnda-ka
   S/he (subject) me(object)   hit (-past)   stick(-with)

   He hit me with a stick

3 Thardaji-rna yukurru   kuju-yi
   bury(-past)   dog   bone(-object)

   The dog buried a bone

4 Ngaju   warli   bilya-rna
   I (object)   snake (subject)   bite(-past)

   The snake bit me

5 Thukutha-nma   mangkuru   ngunhu   kurjarda-wari
   spear (-imperative) kangaroo   that one   spear(-with)

   Spear that roo with a spear

6 Balalyi mayaka-bura waka-na   thaka-ru   nyamina-ku
   then   man(-plural) go(-past) get(-past) dugong(-object)

   In those days men would hunt for dugong

7 Ngayi   yarnima-ru   wirrba-yi   nyinku
   I (subject)   make (-future)   boomerang   you(object)
                                      (-indirect object)

   I'll make you a boomerang

continued...

8 Balu   thaka-ru   ngalikutharnduku   baba-yi
S/he   get(-future)   us two(object inclusive)   water(-object)

He'll get water for us (two)

9 Ngayi   wantharru   mangkurla   marnburra   nyinda-la
I (subject)   put (future)   child   knee   you(subject)   (-location)

I'll put the child on your knee

Notice that the word order is different to English. Words are marked as being subjects or objects, so their order in a sentence isn't as important as it is in English. If we said 'The man bit the dog', it has a different meaning to 'The dog bit the man'. But in Ngarluma you could say **Mayaka yukurru-ku bilya-rna**, or **Mayaka-ku yukurru bilya-rna**, with the suffix **-ku** telling us that the word it is attached to is the object of the sentence.

Using the information in the sentences above, try the following.

What is the Ngarluma word for:

water _____

snake _____

boomerang _____

dugong _____

child _____

stick _____

How would you say:

The dog bit me _____

You will make me a boomerang _____

I bit the snake _____

Now try to make up some other sentences in Ngarluma.

Jane Simpson

Making sense of the words in old wordlists

Making sense of the words in old wordlists

earning a language is more than just learning how the words sound, and what they mean. We need to know how to use the words, how to put them together in sentences. To do this properly you need a grammar of the language. There are very few grammars of the Aboriginal languages that are no longer spoken. There are far more wordlists than grammars, because it is easier to collect a list of words of a language, than it is to work out how to use them in sentences.

But if you have a wordlist of a language, it may give some clues about how to put words together in sentences. Some wordlists include example sentences, and they are very useful sources, but even wordlists without example sentences may contain clues. To make the best use of them you really need to have a speaker and a grammar of a neighbouring language that is closely related.

Understanding the grammar of a language is not easy. However, I will give some examples below of uncovering these clues. I'll use material from two South Australian languages — Kaurna, the language of the Adelaide Plains, and Barngarla, the language of the Eyre Peninsula and north. These languages are quite typical of languages spoken over most of Australia.

Of course, I can only give a sketchy idea of some important characteristics. You might like to look at Colin Yallop's article, The Structure of Australian Aboriginal Languages (1993), for a fuller explanation of some of the ideas touched on here.

ictionaries of Aboriginal languages often have labels for the kinds of words in the dictionary. For instance, in the Barngarla dictionary, there is an entry:

    penyi   S   smart, pain

where S stands for 'substantive' or, as it is more often known, 'noun' — that is, a word which describes a thing or a person. So we know from this that *penyi* doesn't describe an action ('His foot <u>pained</u> him'); it describes a thing ('He felt a sharp <u>pain</u>').

Here is a list of labels for kinds of words:

N, NOM, S	**noun, nominal, substantive**	words for things and people	dog language grammar, girl
V	**verb**	words for actions and states	come, die speak, dig write
ADJ	**adjective**	words describing things and people	big, small innocent
ADV	**adverb**	words describing how an action is carried out	quickly, often happily carefully probably
PRO, PRON	**pronoun**	words that stand instead of nouns	I, you, he she, it

Many Australian Aboriginal languages make an important distinction between two types of verbs:

- verbs where someone does something to someone or something else:

  I *lit* the fire. You are *eating* the fish. The sun *dried* the clothes. I *saw* the elephant.

  In some wordlists these are called TRANSITIVE verbs, or active verbs. They are sometimes abbreviated as: TV, VT or VA.

- verbs where someone or something just is, or becomes something, or does something without involving someone or something else:

  She *ran*. She *died*. The sky *is* dark. The sky darkened.

  In some wordlists these are called INTRANSITIVE verbs, or stative verbs or neutral verbs. They are sometimes abbreviated as: IV, VI, VS or VN

Sometimes wordlists don't include labels, but the English translations give you clues. For instance, in a wordlist of Kaurna pepared by William Wyatt we find:

kanterla	sweat

On its own we cannot tell whether this is a verb or a noun. However, in the rest of the list there are many words like the following:

onye	to laugh
panmeende	to dive
patteende	to thrust into the ground

It seems as though Wyatt tries to translate verbs into English using 'to'. So we can guess that *kanterla* must be a noun and not a verb. And when we look at another word list of Kaurna, that of Teichelmann and Schürmann (1840), we find:

kandarla	S	perspiration, sweat
kandarlangandi	VN	to perspire, to sweat

From this we can tell that our earlier guess was right — *kanterla* means the thing, perspiration, and not the action of sweating. It is a noun, not a verb. We can use it in sentences like, 'Sweat stained his shirt', but not in 'He sweated a lot'. The way to talk about the action is to use *kandarlangandi* — the label VN means that it is an intransitive verb.

But this example raises a new question. Does *kandarlangandi* really mean 'to sweat'? The answer to this is: yes and no. No, it doesn't exactly mean 'to sweat' — that is, you can't use it in a sentence like, 'He doesn't want to sweat'. But yes, it does mean 'sweat'. 'To sweat' is a CITATION FORM. A citation form is the conventional way a word is represented in a dictionary. For instance, we know that 'write', 'writes', 'wrote', 'written', 'writing', 'to write' all belong together; they share a meaning; they are all forms of the same word. Likewise we know that 'book' and 'books' belong together. However, suppose we make separate entries for them in a dictionary:

write	make letters on paper
writes	someone makes letters on paper
wrote	made letters on paper

written	made letters on paper
to write	to make letters on paper
writing	making letters on paper
book	written or printed work
books	written or printed work

You can see that there is a lot of repetition. So usually dictionary makers choose one form as a citation form to represent the whole word. In English, we normally use WRITE, SWEAT, PERSPIRE, etc as the citation forms.

write	to make letters on paper ('writes', 'wrote' 'written', 'writing')
book	written or printed work

Dictionary-makers also often choose one form to represent the meaning. For verbs in English this is often the 'to' form, 'to make letters' in the example.

Now, what about *kandarlangandi?* Teichelmann and Schürmann represent its meaning with the 'to' form, 'to perspire'. But Kaurna doesn't have a 'to' form like English. *Kandarlangandi* actually means 'Someone is' — or 'I am', or 'you are' — 'sweating'. We know this from the grammar. Verbs ending in *-ndi* or *-ne* or *-ni* in Kaurna mean that the action is happening now, in the present; that is, *-ndi* or *-ne* or *-ni* express the present tense. So, dictionary makers are using the present tense as the citation form.

A good wordlist will use the same form as the citation form all the way through. However, earlier recorders did not always understand the material they were getting. For example, Wyatt gives us:

kokaritte   to scratch the skin

This word ends in -*tte*. It does not look like the present tense forms -*ndi* or -*ne* or -*ni* . In fact there are at least two endings sometimes written -*tti* in Kaurna. Adding one of these endings to a verb means something like 'Someone scratched himself' (action that happened in the past: past tense). Adding the other means 'Don't scratch yourself' (telling someone not to do something: negative imperative).

Wyatt also gives us:

bookoo-bookoo   to shave

This word seems to be doubled and it doesn't contain the ending -*ndi*. In fact, when we look at Teichelmann and Schürmann, this word turns out to be an adjective:

bukko-bukko   ADJ   bald

It is easy to understand how confusion arose. Here's another example, from Williams, another early recorder of Kaurna:

we-ril-lah   to make haste

The ending does not look like the present tense verb ending at all. In fact, looking at Teichelmann and Schürmann we find:

wirrilla   ADV   quickly, hastily, fast

Perhaps someone said to Williams: *Wirrilla!* 'Quickly!' And he understood this as 'Make haste!'

Confusion over what is a verb can also go the other way. The next example, from Wyatt, is actually a verb, as we can see from looking at Teichelmann and Schürmann:

boolyoreende   blue, dark, cloudy [Wyatt]

pulyorendi   to be or become, black, dark [T&S]

How did such a confusion arise? It probably arose because Kaurna, like most Australian Aboriginal languages, has no special separate word for 'is', 'am', 'are'. To say, 'It is dark', all one has to say is something like *Pulyorendi*. Wyatt probably interpreted this as 'dark', rather than as 'It is dark'.

Let's look now at some properties of types of words that may come up in wordlists.

Types of words

Pronouns

Many Australian Aboriginal languages have different words for 'you', 'we' and 'they', depending on how many people there are:

Pitjantjatjara

you (one person)	**nyuntu**		
you two	**nyupali**	we two	**ngali**
you mob	**nyura**	we mob	**nganarna**

That's one of the reasons why in the wordlists you will often find several words for 'we' and 'you'. Sometimes the older wordlists make a distinction with 'you' — they use 'you' for more than one person , and 'thou' for one person. Sometimes they add notes like dual (two people) or plural (more than one person or more than two people, depending on whether there is a dual in the language).

Many Australian Aboriginal languages don't have separate words for 'she', 'he' and 'it'. Here's an example from Barngarla, in which *padlo* can mean 'she', 'he', 'it'.

> **Padlo ngai mai kutta nungkunnarru**
> She did not give me food,
>
> or   he did not give me food,
>
> or   it did not give me food
>
> | | |
> |---|---|
> | **ngai** | me |
> | **mai** | food |
> | **kutta** | not |
> | **nungkunnarru** | gave |

Another reason why you may find several forms of pronouns is that Australian Aboriginal languages very often use endings to tell you who is doing what to who. In English, the order of words shows who is doing what to who: 'Mary bit the dog'; 'The dog bit Mary'. In most Aboriginal languages, endings on words do this. Here are some examples from Kaurna to show this:

> | | |
> |---|---|
> | **Gadla padlondi** | The fire is dying |
> | **gadla** | fire |
> | **padlondi** | is dying |

> | | |
> |---|---|
> | **Gadla-rlo ngai ngadli** | The fire has burnt me |
> | **ngai** | me |
> | **ngadli** | has burnt |

Munangka gadla parra ngatto

I will light first the fire

munangka	first
parra	will light
atto~ngatto	I (for transitive verbs like 'light')

Ngai yaintya wandeota

I shall sleep here

ngai	I (for intransitive verbs like 'lie', 'die')
yaintya	here
wandeota	will lie

You can see here that Kaurna uses the same word *ngai* for 'I' when there is an intransitive verb: 'I sleep', 'I die'; and for 'me' when it is the object of a transitive verb, 'it has burnt me'. It uses a different word *ngatto* for 'I' when it is the subject of a transitive verb, 'I will light the fire'.

The result is that in early wordlists you often find two words for 'I', and you often find the same word used for 'I' and 'me'. Early recorders often found this very confusing. If this is still confusing for you, read the article by Yallop mentioned earlier.

Exercise

Look at the words for 'fire' in the three sentences above.

Which form behaves like **ngai** and which like **ngatto**?

▶

Discussion (don't read this until you've had a think)

You add **-rlo** to **gadla** when it acts as the subject of a transitive verb 'The fire burnt me'. So **gadla-rlo** acts like **ngatto**. And **gadla** on its own acts like **ngai**. We call endings like **-rlo** ERGATIVE. Many Australian languages have ergative endings.

Nouns and adjectives

In most Australian Aboriginal languages there are no words for 'a', 'an' and 'the'. Look at the following example from Barngarla.

Barngarla

> **Wariyoko bamburritawo murdliringi**
>
> The ship is stationary in the calm
>
> > **bamburritawo**   is stationary
> >
> > **wariyoko**   ship
> >
> > **murdliringi**   in calm weather

The English translation has 'the' twice. The Barngarla has no word matching 'the'.

Nouns and adjectives are often interchangeable. That is, the same word can be used to name a thing or to describe something like that thing. For instance, the Kaurna word *gadla* for 'fire' can also mean 'hot'.

In English we have to say whether we are talking about one thing ('book', 'dog', 'child') or more than one thing ('books', 'dogs', 'children'). In many Aboriginal languages, words can be marked for whether there are one, two (dual), or more than two (plural), but only if knowing the number of things is important in understanding what is going on. It is usually important to know the number of people involved, but less important to know the number of things (eg fish).

Barngarla

yura	man
yuralbelli	two men
yurarri	men
marra	hand
marralbelli	two hands

Barngarla

Kuyanga yurarri muwarritanna

The men are employed in (catching) fish

kuya	fish
muwarritanna	be employed in

In this sentence it is important to know that a particular group of men is fishing, and so *yura* has the plural marker *-rri*. In the next sentence, however, the speaker is merely saying that anyone's head would ache, and so *yura* has no marker.

Barngarla

Nunno yura kakka puttungkutu

You make people's heads ache

nunno	you

kakka	head
puttungkutu	make ache

(The ending *-tu* on the verb actually means 'do something now', ie present tense).

Sometimes words are doubled to show that there is more than one thing. So in Warumungu, a language of Central Australia, *pulkka* means 'old person', *pulka-pulkka* means 'several old people'.

In wordlists you often find doubled words. Sometimes they mean that there is more than one thing, as we just saw. On verbs, they often mean that the action is done more than once. Often new adjectives can be made from nouns by doubling. Or nouns can be made from adjectives by doubling.

Kaurna

karro	blood	**karro-karro**	red
tammi	flat	**tammi-ammi**	plate

Barngarla

yallu	flame	**yalluyallu**	red hot

Often new words can be made by joining words together:

Barngarla

yerru	whirl	**yerruwarri**	whirlwind
warri	wind	**warri-kalyoru**	bleak wind
kalyoru	bleak, chill		

Exercise

Have a look at the following words from Schürmann's Parnkalla dictionary. What can you say about them?

palta marraba	without clothing
gadla marraba	without fire
mai marraba	having no food, destitute
kauo marraba	without water

Discussion (don't read this until you've had a go)

From these we can guess that **marraba** means 'not having, without'. But unlike the Kaurna **tinna** this time **marraba** is written as a separate word. However, unlike 'without' in English, it has to follow the other word. ■

Often new words can be made by adding endings. Look at the following Kaurna words from Teichelmann and Schürmann's dictionary:

turnkitinna	not having clothes
maiitinna	without food
parutinna	without meat
gadlatinna	without wood
kartotinna	having no wife

From these we can guess that -*tinna* means 'not having, without'.

It can be used to form more abstract meanings:

turlatinna	not quarrelling	**turla**	anger
tiatinna	toothless, blunt	**tia**	tooth
mokatinna	stupid, silly	**moka**	brain

Another very common ending is shown in the following example from Barngarla:

kaya ilka	provided with spears, armed
kakko ilka	having a head, obstinate
mai-ilkanna	having food, rich
mankailkanna	having dots, a grown up man (**manka** means 'dots, tattoo scars')

Lots of languages have an ending meaning 'having, provided with'.

So, when you look at a wordlist, try and look for common patterns. They may help you find ways of making sentences in the language.

Many Australian languages use endings to show meanings like 'in', 'on', 'from', 'to' etc. Here's a sentence from Kaurna to show you how it works.

Karra ngai padne Yultiwirraanna

Up to the Stringy-bark forest will I go

karra	high, up
ngai	I
padne	will go
yulti	stringybark
wirra	forest

You can see that -*anna* expresses the idea of 'to'.

So you normally wouldn't expect to find separate words in wordlists with meanings like 'to' or 'in' or 'for'. Moreover, the usual citation form for a noun is without any endings at all. But sometimes in wordlists you will find forms with endings. For example, many languages also often have an ending meaning 'for' or 'wanting', as in 'I went for firewood', 'I am hungry for food'. This ending sometimes turns up in wordlists on words for 'food' or 'water'. So in Wyatt's wordlist we find:

mayeecha	hungry

This is made up of the word *mayi* 'food', and an ending meaning 'for'.

Now look at the following examples from Wyatt's Kaurna wordlist.

werle	house
werlingga	at or in a house
yo:ko	a ship
yoko:ngga	in a ship
wingko	the breath
wingko:ngga	the place on which a man dies which receives his breath
moonto	belly
moonttoongga pallo:ne	a miscarriage
(pallo:ne	is another form of *padlondi*, means 'to die'.)

You can see that the -*ngga* ending here means something like 'at', 'in'. And here is an example sentence from Teichelmann and Schürmann's dictionary backing up this idea.

Nantungga ba padnendi	He goes on horseback
ba	she, he, it
nantu	horse
padnendi	is going

Looking at placenames often reveals this type of ending, because very often the early recorders recorded the name of a place plus ending. Here is a list of placenames from Wyatt.

Ungke Perre	Field's River
Ungke perringga	Onkaparinga River
Willa willungga	Rodney's country, from Onkaparinga to Willunga, and south of it
Auldingga	Aldinga
Maippungga	Myponga
Korra weerungga	Districts of the Adelaide tribe
Peelta werlingga	Districts of the Adelaide tribe

You can see they all have this -*ngga* ending.

Verbs

We have already looked at two very important properties of verbs. The first is whether they are transitive or intransitive. The second is that the citation form is very often the present tense.

Verbs often have endings like the present tense to show when an action or event took place. We have seen the present tense endings in Kaurna and Barngarla. Normally those are the most likely endings to find in a wordlist. But sometimes you may find other endings. For instance, in Wyatt's Kaurna wordlists we find the following:

kutteen	to bring, fetch or carry
kutteendo	bring thou
peenjáne	to write
peenjánto	write thou
wantándo	do not do that, desist

You can see an ending that looks like *-nto* or *-ndo*. And the meaning appears to be a command. From the use of 'thou' rather than 'you', we can guess that it is a command addressed to one person. Notice that the verbs all look transitive. When we learn that the word for 'you' (one person) is *nindo* when it is the subject of a transitive verb, we can guess that *-nto* and *-ndo* are short forms of *nindo*.

Let's look some more now at the two types of verb, transitive and intransitive. Take a sentence like 'I hit myself'. Doing something to oneself is called REFLEXIVE. This is halfway between the transitive type (because someone is doing something to someone) and the intransitive type (because the person is doing something to themselves, not to someone else). Some languages treat it as transitive, and some treat it as intransitive. Some languages mark verbs in special ways to show that they are being used reflexively.

Look at the following examples from Teichelmann and Schürmann's Kaurna dictionary.

bakkendi	VA	to cut
bakkirendi	VR	to cut oneself
kaltendi	VA	to ask; command
kaltirendi	VR	to ask for oneself
kattendi	VA	to carry; to fetch
kattirendi	VR	to fetch for oneself
kudlendi	VA	to wash; clean
kudlirendi	VR	to wash oneself

In a modern spelling system *bakkendi* might be written *pakinti*, and so on. Now there are several things to notice about this list. First, all the words end in *-ndi (-nti)*. This ending means that the action is happening now; that is, it expresses present tense.

Second, some of the verbs are said to be VA, and some are said to be VR. All the VA verbs represent things that a person does to something or someone else: one cuts a person or a piece of bread, one asks a person for something, one carries someone or something, one washes someone or something. They are all transitive verbs.

All the VR verbs represent things that a person does to himself, or for himself. In Kaurna they are all treated as intransitive verbs. Moreover, they all have an extra *r* in them. We can break up a word like *bakkirendi* as:

paki-ri-nti	She is cutting herself
cut-self-PRESENT or	He is cutting himself...
	and so on

Exercise

Have a look at the following words from Schürmann's Parnkalla dictionary. What can you say about them?

warringarriti		to cut oneself
yerlingarriti	V	to hide oneself
irata	V	to keep off, defend, protect
irangarriti	V	to disengage oneself
pullungarriti	V	to wipe oneself, wash
pullutu	V	to wipe, brush, sweep
kantyiti	VA	to lead, conduct
kantyingarriti	V	to carry about with one, as food

Discussion (don't read this until you've had a go)

First, all the meanings of the words look like verb meanings. Moreover, some of them are labelled V and one is labelled VA. We can guess that the VA one, **kantyiti**, is transitive, both because of its meaning and because of the label. We can't say anything much about the others because V could stand for verb — regardless of whether it is transitive or intransitive.

Second, the words all end in **-ti** or **-tu** or **-ta**. This looks like an ending.

Third, several of the words have **ngarri** in them, and their meanings seem to involve doing something to oneself or for oneself.

continued...

> Fourth, some pairs of words seem related: **pullutu** 'to wipe',
> **pullungarriti** 'to wipe oneself'. These words have **pullu** in
> common. We can guess from this that we can break down these
> words as follows:
>
> **pullu-tu**   wipe-?
>
> **pullu-ngarri-ti**   wipe-self-?
>
> Now we can guess that **-tu** appears when the word ends with **u**, and
> **-ti** when the word ends with **i**. What happens when the word ends
> with **a**? Why, we get **ta: irata.** ■

So, if you see a lot of words with meanings like 'cut oneself' or 'shave oneself' in a wordlist, have a good look and see if you can find something in common between the words — like the *-ri-* in Kaurna.

I said earlier that Kaurna, like other Australian languages, has several ways of expressing the ideas that English expresses through words like 'is', 'am', 'are'.

First, they may just put words together without a joining 'is', 'am', 'are'. Here are two example sentences, one from Kaurna, and one from Schürmann's dictionary of Parnkalla [Barngarla].

Kaurna

Tindo natta wongarta	The sun is now in the west
tindo	sun
natta	now
wongarta	west

Barngarla

Karkalla ngunya	The figs are overripe
karkalla	native fig
ngunya	overripe

Second they may create special words meaning 'to be something' by adding endings. Look at the following words:

karrarendi	VN	to be proud; haughty
kurturendi	VN	to be or look sad, sorry, dejected
manyarendi	VN	to be cold
mentamentarendi	VN	to be wearied; tired

You can see that they all end in -rendi. We know that -ndi is the present tense. What is -re? It is an ending which makes verbs meaning 'be something'. So *manya* means 'the cold, rain', and *manyarendi* means 'Someone is cold'. You can also see that they are all labelled VN. They are all intransitive verbs.

Notice something odd — this *re* looks exactly like the *re* that we saw earlier in Kaurna when we were talking about reflexive verbs. And indeed it is.

Add *re* to a transitive verb like 'cut' and you get a reflexive verb, 'cut oneself'. Add *re* to a noun like 'cold' and you get an intransitive verb 'be cold'.

What does this mean? It means that the reflexive verbs are actually a special type of intransitive verb in Kaurna. Lots (but not all) Aboriginal languages work like Kaurna. They have special ways of making intransitive verbs, and of making reflexives.

Exercise

In the last exercise we looked at some Barngarla verbs made with **ngarri**. Here are some more words made with **ngarri**.

Have a look at the following words from Schürmann's Parnkalla dictionary. What can you say about them?

yurre mantyarri	in good humour, glad, merry
yurre mantyarringarriti	to be pleased, in good humour

Now have a look at these words. What can you say about them?

kallata	V	to call, hail
kallangarriti	V	to call to each other
paitya karata	VA	to commence a quarrel
		(**paitya** means 'fight')
karangarriti	V	to quarrel

Discussion (don't read this until you've had a go)

yurre mantyarri looks like an adjective, while **yurre mantyarringarriti** looks like a verb — it has the **-ti** ending we saw earlier. We can guess that **ngarri** doesn't only make reflexive verbs, it also makes verbs out of adjectives.

Second, **kallangarriti** has the meaning 'do something to each other'. This is a special kind of action — you do something to someone and they do the same thing back to you. It is often called RECIPROCAL action. Languages often treat reciprocal actions in the

continued…

◄ same way that they treat reflexive actions — and Barngarla seems to be doing the same. Barngarla uses the suffix **-ngarri** for both reflexive and reciprocal actions.

What about the last verb **karangarriti** ? Why does it have **ngarri**? There's no adjective, there's no 'self' and there's no 'each other' in the definition. The answer is that 'quarrel' is really shorthand for 'quarrel with each other'. So it too is a reciprocal verb.

Notice by the by that **karata** is said to be VA while **karangarriti** is said to be V. This means **karata** is transitive. We might suspect that **karangarriti** is intransitive. But we don't have enough evidence yet to be sure about this. ■

Languages also often have special ways of making transitive verbs. Here's an example from Barngarla.

mauurrurriti	V	to be black
mauurruringutu	VA	to make dark, blacken
mirkarriti	V	to be taken by surprise
mirkarringutu	V	to surprise, frighten
murreriti	V	to be healthy, well
murreringutu	VA	to make well, mend
ngalgutu		to eat
ngalgungutu	VA	to make or let eat
ngallanniti		to become large, grow
ngallanningutu		to make grow, increase

nganiti	to return
nganingutu	to send, carry back

You can see that these words form pairs: one ends in *-ngutu* and the other doesn't. The one ending in *-ngutu* seems to mean something like 'to make something, be or do something'. This is sometimes called a causative ending. Lots of Australian languages have causative endings, and they make transitive verbs. ◼

An example of
how not to use historical sources

After having read this far the reader should be aware that historical sources generally leave much to be desired in accurately reflecting the languages they are trying to record.

A recent publication (Gerritsen 1994) has used a number of arguments in an attempt to prove that shipwrecked Dutch sailors settled on the west coast of Australia in the seventeenth century.

The author uses old sources for the languages of the area without understanding their flaws, and suggests for example that the use of **kn** at the beginning of words written in these records shows a similarity to Dutch (in fact, this is a common way of recording the sound **ng** at the beginning of words, where it does not occur in English). He also suggests that the word for water in the region should look something like **ngapa** or **gapa**, and that the recorded form is **howa** or **owwa**. It is well known that a neighbouring language can change sounds like **p** to **w** between vowels; this has happened further north in the Pilbara languages Ngarluma and Yindjibarndi, where forms in Ngarluma like **maparn** are said **mawarn** in Yindjibarndi.

Making these mistakes with old sources is bad enough, but, what's more, there is good recent work in the languages of the area (eg Austin 1992), a handbook which lists available work (Thieberger 1993) and a language centre operating in Geraldton which could have provided accurate information. ∎

Rob
Amery

Learning and reviving
a language from
historical sources

Learning and reviving a language from historical sources

here is a common notion that language learning means learning vocabulary (words), as if all we need to do to learn a language is 'swallow the dictionary'. It is a bit like giving someone a collection of cogs, flywheels, hands, casing and clock face and saying, 'Here's your clock'. Perhaps even more important than learning vocabulary is learning what makes the language tick — the grammar. We need to know how to string the words together to make meaningful utterances and how to put sentences together to form a coherent story or conversation.

It is good to have long-term goals when learning a language. It is even better to establish short-term goals that are achievable given your situation and resources. Is the aim to produce fluent speakers who can use the language in all areas of life? Or is it to learn some of the language? Is it to reclaim one's linguistic heritage and to demonstrate some active knowledge of that heritage?

What are the expectations? And are they realistic? There are some things we can do and some things we can't do. With the best will in the world, in many situations the language loss has been so great that there's very little we can do to reverse that. However, in some situations (eg Kaurna), there's a surprising amount we can do, including:

- retrieval of language from historical sources
- linguistic reconstruction
- filling in the gaps.

aurna is the original language of Adelaide and the
Adelaide Plains stretching from Crystal Brook in the
north to Cape Jervis in the south. The Kaurna people were
decimated (by smallpox and other diseases) and dispersed away
from their country in the early contact period. By 1860,
according to the historical record, few Kaurna remained. Ivaritji,
the last person of full Kaurna descent, died in 1929, whilst the
second-last person of full descent died in 1907, and the last male
in 1897. However, Kaurna people and Kaurna identity have
survived. Kaurna people have been returning to Adelaide this
century, a Kaurna heritage committee has been set up and
Kaurna identity has been firmly re-established. In recent times,
Kaurna history and some aspects of Kaurna culture have been
introduced into schools within the Aboriginal Studies
curriculum. A Kaurna dreaming track, the Tjilbruke Trail, which
traverses the southern portion of Kaurna territory, has been
marked out. Kaurna is coming to have a higher profile within
public life in Adelaide.

**A Kaurna
case study**

What remains of the Kaurna language?

There are no fluent speakers of the Kaurna language remaining.
In fact, the few Kaurna words known were, until recently,
identified without exception by their speakers as Narrunga from
nearby Yorke Peninsula. The number of such known words is not
large, but includes *tidna* 'foot', *kalta* 'sleepy lizard', *angki* 'woman'.

Narrunga and Kaurna were in fact very closely related, with many words being shared by both languages.

Fortunately, reasonably good quality written documentation of the Kaurna language remains. Two German missionaries, Teichelmann and Schürmann, published *Outlines of a Grammar, Vocabulary, and Phraseology of the Aboriginal Language of South Australia, Spoken by the Natives in and for Some Distance around Adelaide* in 1840, after just eighteen months' work on the language. In 1982 this book was reprinted as a facsimile edition. It contains a sketch grammar, a vocabulary of some 2000 words and about 200 translated sentences.

Pages from Teichelmann and Schürmann (1840).

69

Nammurlinyanna   ngaidyurna   Of this age were my children
madli   when they died
Ngaityuitti kokato;   ngaidyo First, I will dig my land; when
manni yerta wandeota, ninko-   that is done, I will dig for you
anni kokato
Ngando parnukko bukketidla Who will fetch her two buckets
katteota kauwidla? — Kuma   of water? — Any person may
meyu kauwaima   come and do it
Ngatto ngurrintyilla, ninna yung- Were I permitted to throw,
kama   you (I) would give (the game)
Paintya ninna wandi.—Ne, yaint- Lie there.—Yes, there I shall
ya ngai wandeota   lie down (or sleep)
Pulyunna meyu tittappeurti, Don't hang the black man,
pindi meyu nurruttoai   the European be not charmed
                                             (or enchanted)
Pindi meyunna ngarraitye pad- Plenty of Europeans will die by
lota nurrutilo. Windarlo, ka-   the charm. Let (the natives)
yarlo kudla pammareanna mar-   themselves spear the murderer
punna   with the wirado or kaya
Pa ngaintya wǎnggi? What did he say?
Painingga purlaityehdi meyurla Formerly, only two men had
tittappe; natta pirianda; kut-   been hanged; now it is evident
tena tittappeurti kutteni nur-   don't hang again; don't spear
ruttoai adli; purrutye adiu   again; lest we all die. The flesh
padlettoai. Kudla mai tunki.   decompose (i.e. be eaten;) the
neta; pikeurlo ngarkota   pig will eat it
Pia ngaintya pia, yerrarend' ai Whatever it is, I am pleased
Pulyunna meyurlo yakko yailtya The black man did not know
pindi meyu budnitina   that the white man would
                                             come
Parnaintya—parna; parniappin- Those are they—those, I have
dunna   them
Parni kattindo Fetch it; carry it hither
Parniappindo }   Hand it hither
Parnimanmando }
Parni yungcndo Give it; reach it hither
Padneadli; turlarla, adli nur- He is angry; let him alone,
rottoai   that he does not kick
Pirriurlo atto tidna kokandi I scratch the foot

8

THIRD PERSON:

	Sing.	Dual.	Plur.
Nom.	Pa, he, she, or it,	purla, they two,	parna, they
Gen.	Parnu or Parnu-ko, of him, }	purlako, of them two,	parnako, of them
Dat.	Pänni or Padni, to him, }	purlanni, to them two,	parnanni, to them
Acc.	Pa, them,	purla, them two,	parna, them
Act.	Padlo, he, &c., } the agent		

NOTE.—Each person, number, and case, may take the restrictive affix, *ndi*, which corresponds with the English adverbs *only* or *but*, or the adjective *alone*, or frequently with a personal pronoun terminating in the syllable *self*; for instance—*Ngattondi mappeota*—I alone (or myself) will do it. *Ninnandi mantarti*—But do not you lie.

To the active case of each person and number, the terminations *ityа* and *ityangga* may be added, thus :—.

	Sing.	Dual.	Plur.
1.—Ngattaitya,	ngadlilitya,	ngadlulitya
2.—Nindaitya,	niwadlitya,	naalitya
3.—Padlaitya,	purlalitya,	parnalitya
1.—Ngattaityangga,	ngadlilityangga,	ngadlulityangga
2.—Nindaityangga,	niwadlityangga,	naalityangga
3.—Padlaityangga,	purlalityangga,	parnalityangga

When *itya* is affixed to these pronouns, they must be rendered by the prepositions *to* or *for*; as, *Wanti ninna murreota? Nindaitya*—Whither are you going? To you. *Ninna yakko ngattaitya morpulaii*—You have not worked for me.

When *ityangga* is affixed, they can be rendered sometimes by *with* or *to*, or by the accusative; as, *Ngadlulityangga pa wandeota*—He will stay with us. *Naalityangga ngai pudlori*—I have told it to you. *Nindaityangga ngai marngari*—I have asked you.

An additional unpublished manuscript by Teichelmann (1857) contains a more comprehensive vocabulary and additional phrases and sentences. It was located in a library in South Africa, having been lodged there by South Australia's former Governor, Captain Grey. These two vocabularies are available on disk; they are the two main sources on the Kaurna language. In addition, several short wordlists were compiled by other observers.

Unfortunately, few texts were ever recorded. To date, only two short letters written by Kaurna children attending the Native Location School have been found. The first, dated 1841, was sent to Governor Gawler and was signed by a number of the children. The second, dated 1845, was sent to Governor Grey and his wife.

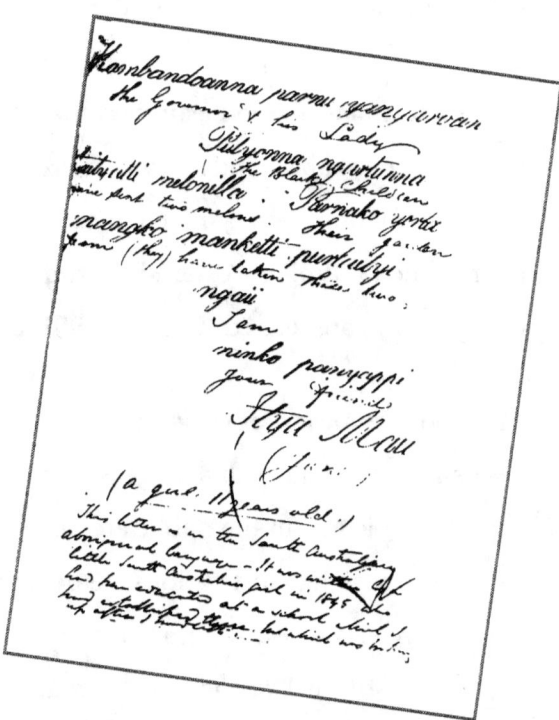

Letter written by Itya Mau, 1845.

Teichelmann and Schürmann (1840) were generally consistent in the way in which they wrote Kaurna. However, they missed some important distinctions between different kinds of sounds (eg between interdental and retroflex consonants), and they over-represented the vowels. Whilst their description of the language is incomplete, there is enough material in it (combining the grammar outlines complete with pronoun paradigms, nominal affix charts etc, with the vocabulary and the sentences provided) to create new sentences and write or translate a wide range of materials.

Kaurna belongs to the Pama-Nyungan language family. Fortunately, Adnyamathanha in the Flinders Ranges and Pitjantjatjara in the north of South Australia are not too far distant relatives. Where there are gaps or uncertainties in relation to grammar and meanings of words, we are able to look to these better known and still vibrant related languages to aid in reconstruction. Twenty-nine per cent of the vocabulary of Kaurna and Pintupi (a Western Desert dialect closely related to Pitjantjatjara) are related (O'Grady 1991, pers comm).

The public function of language

In Adelaide, the Kaurna language is coming to perform a very important role within the public arena:

- Aboriginal institutions are being named with Kaurna names — Kura Yerlo Council Inc, Tandanya Cultural Institute, Warriapendi Alternative School and Inbarendi College;

- Speeches are being given in Kaurna — for instance, at the opening of Yaitya Warra Wodli, the South Australian Aboriginal Languages Centre, in February 1992 (see p 164);

- Kaurna is used in songs sung at special occasions — for instance, at the opening of Yaitya Warra Wodli and NAIDOC Week. Greetings, leavetakings and terms of address have already become well established at Kaurna Plains School where the Kaurna language program is operating. Speeches of welcome in Kaurna are almost routine now at public gatherings where Kaurna Plains School is involved. Nungas take pride in being able to use their language in public;

- Kaurna signs have appeared at the University of South Australia in the Faculty of Aboriginal Studies — for instance, for the enquiries desk, lecture rooms, conference room and toilets. More recently many Kaurna signs have been posted at the Aboriginal Education Unit within the Department of Education.

What to do with the materials?

What can you do once you have worked through the historical materials and have a wordlist or dictionary or texts in the language?

Songs

Songs are a great starting point. It is very easy to learn to sing songs in a foreign language, especially if the tune is already known and the general meaning of the song is clear. This has proved to be very effective in Adelaide. In time, through singing the songs, the sound system of the language begins to sink in and people begin to develop more of a feeling for the language in a non-threatening and fun way. Nursery rhymes are great with little kids.

Kaurna translation of the children's song *Kookaburra Sits in the Old Gum Tree.*

Ngungana Karrangga Tikketti
(Kookaburra Sits in the old Gum Tree)
Kaurna Version by Rob Amery 14/11/91

Ngungana karrangga tikketti

Mengki mengki pa wirra mattanya

Karnke! Ngungana karnke! Ngungana

Ninna kalyamarroalya.

English Version
Kookaburra sits in the old gum tree
Merry merry king of the bush is he
Laugh! Kookaburra laugh! Kookaburra
Gay your life must be.

Vocabulary

ngungana	'kookaburra'
karra	'red gum tree'
karrangga	'in the red gum tree'
tikkandi	'sitting'
tikketti	'habitually sits' (see T&S p16)
mengki	'laughter; joy; joke'
pa	'he, she, it'
wirra	'wood; forest; bush'
mattanya	'owner; proprieter; master'
karnkendi	'laughing'
karnke	'laugh!'
ninna	'you'
kalyamarro	'lively; active; gay'
-alya	Particle which expresses surprise or wonder (See T&S p 23)

Make the sessions active

It is always easier to talk about something in front of you. And it is much easier for the language learner to follow what's being said if the dialogue is about something that is here and now and concrete. Don't be afraid to gather up some artifacts, foodstuffs, leaves, branches, stones, water etc, and take them into the language learning session. It may be somewhat artificial, but these items can be easily passed around. With them you can practise requests, commands, statements or commentary and other basic structures in the language. You will find these basic structures (eg 'Pass me the ___' or 'Give the ___ to ___' or 'Where is the ___?') to be very useful in all kinds of situations.

It is a good idea to use our bodies as much as possible. Commands such as 'Stand up!', 'Come here!', 'Go over there!', 'Sit down!', 'Lie down!', 'Give the ___ to ___!' are very useful. If they are accompanied by body movement fulfilling the request or command, the expressions and language structures will sink in and be remembered much better. The actions become associated with the expressions. One language teaching methodology, Total Physical Response (TPR), bases its entire methodology on this.

Use names and relationship terms

In addition to personal names, Kaurna is fortunate in that it has birth order names. These names are readily applicable — anyone can use them. It appears that the birth order names were

Exercise

Split up into language groups and have a go at writing a version of *Heads, Shoulders, Knees and Toes, I'm Nunga and I'm Proud of It* or *Kookaburra Sits in the Old Gum Tree* in your own language. If you have the body part terms documented, then *Heads, Shoulders, Knees and Toes* is easy to do, even if you don't have any sentence structures written down or known in your language.

Leigh Newton's song *Show Me Where the Names Go* is similar in terms of the Kaurna content. ▪

the usual form of address. Similarly, subsection names or 'skin names' could well have been documented in the language you are teaching/learning. Use them at every opportunity.

Relationship terms like auntie, uncle, brother, sister, are good words to learn early on because they can be used so readily. Some of these relationship terms have already come back into common usage in Kaurna — at least around Kaurna Plains School.

Use common expressions and formulaic language

Learn greetings, leavetakings and other set expressions that can be used as a unit. To begin speaking Kaurna, it is very useful to learn words like *ne* 'yes', *ko* 'OK', *yakko* 'no', *marni* 'good', *wointye* 'maybe', *yakka alya* 'I'm sorry', *ngaityo yungandalya* 'thank you' (lit 'my brother'!) and particles such as *alya* which express surprise. All these words and phrases can be used as stand-alone utterances. One doesn't need a strong grasp of the language to use these expressions appropriately and thus begin to use Kaurna actively. Requests, commands and other expressions are also often used. Making a point of using them at every possible opportunity helps to develop confidence in learning and using the language.

Create a language-rich environment

Use signs and posters to reinforce the language structures being learnt. At Kaurna Plains School, the staff have put signs on the front door *Ninna Marni?* 'How are you?' as you go in, and

Nakkiota! 'See you later' on the back of the door as you leave. Labels for concrete items in the immediate environment can assist with the learning of vocabulary.

Use the language outside of formal session times

Lunchtime or morning tea is a good time to practice the language you are learning. Develop expressions for:

Pass me the _____

This is nice chicken/meat/bread

Would you like a cup of tea? Do you take milk? Sugar?

You can use these same expressions every day. Make an effort to use the language at home, even if you only use it in a few basic expressions for a start. If possible, try to use more than just words.

Try to think in the language

Make yourselves familiar with the materials that you have on the language. Get a good idea of what kinds of words and language structures have been documented. Instead of trying to translate difficult passages from English, choose topics and expressions for which you have the vocabulary and language structures.

Some things will be expressed very differently in your language to the way they might be said in English. In Kaurna for instance, one says *Ngaityo yungandalya* lit 'Oh! My brother!' where English would use 'Thank you'. And presumably other relationship terms (eg *yakkana* 'sister') would be used instead of *yunga* 'brother' in this expression.

Learn to make new words

Look at the common patterns in the language for forming words. By using the right endings (or suffixes) or combining two words to make compounds, you will be able to construct many new words for new concepts. All languages do this. English for instance uses an *-er* suffix attached to verbs to talk about the person who performs the action (eg driver, rider, drinker) or the thing that does the action (eg computer, wringer, cutter). Likewise, Aboriginal languages usually have suffixes that do the same job as the *-er* suffix in English. They also typically have suffixes meaning 'having', 'without', 'associated with' or 'belonging to'. In Kaurna we have developed several new terms on the basis of existing patterns. These new terms include: *padnipadnitti* 'car' from *padnendi* 'to travel'; *karrikarritti* 'aeroplane' from *karrendi* 'to fly'; and *mukamuka karndo* 'computer' (lit 'lightning brain'). Fortunately, many new terms are documented in the Kaurna sources, so we have a good idea of how Kaurna people referred to new things and new concepts back in 1840.

Often the meaning of an existing word is extended or widened to include new objects of similar appearance or function. For instance, according to the 1840 source, the Kaurna word for 'blood' *karro* was extended to refer also to 'wine'; *pari* 'maggot' was extended to refer to 'rice'; *tarlti* 'wing, feather' was used also for 'pen'.

It is worth looking at how 'strong' Aboriginal languages incorporate new concepts into the language. See Simpson (1985), Amery (1986) and O'Grady (1960) for discussion of this in Warumungu, Pintupi and Nyangumarda.

Don't be afraid to borrow words. All languages borrow to a greater or lesser extent. It may be preferable to borrow from neighbouring Aboriginal languages instead of English. In the early contact period, many languages throughout South Australia and Central Australia have borrowed the Kaurna word *nanto* for 'horse'. *Nanto* originally meant 'male kangaroo'. Many languages in eastern Australia have borrowed the word *yarraman* 'horse' from one of the languages spoken around Sydney in NSW.

Using written materials

It is probably not a good idea to base your program too much on literature and written materials. You will probably want the main focus of the program to be oral. However, written materials can be useful to reinforce language learning, especially in situations where little of the language is known in the community.

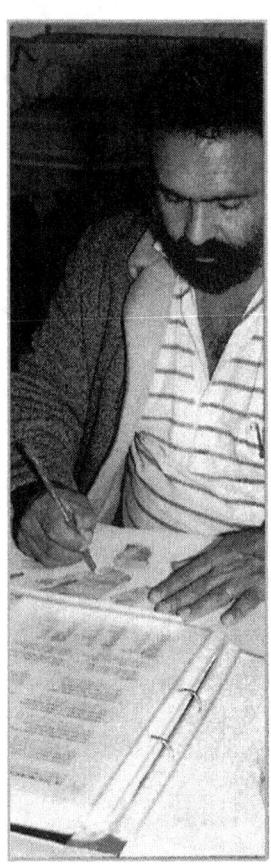

Nelson Varcoe illustrating his story book and the Kaurna song book.

Big books, charts and posters are especially useful. The production of high-quality glossy books can help to increase the status of the language. People are more likely to want to use them if they are attractive and professional looking. They can give the community and children something tangible that they can be proud of. We have translated a popular children's story, *Tucker's Mob,* into Kaurna. In addition, a proposal has been put forward to translate the Tjilbruke Dreaming (currently available in English, see Edwards 1971) back into Kaurna.

The Story of the Falling Star (Jones 1989) and *Narrunga, Kaurna and Ngarrindjeri Songs* (Ngarrindjeri, Narrunga and Kaurna Languages Project 1990) are particularly good examples of literature that can become the focus of community pride in the languages. Writing stories that involve the language learners can be fun. Take a series of photos around a common theme (eg a trip to an important site or place, a fishing expedition, looking after a pet joey, carving emu eggs, or chickens hatching out). Then you can easily write the story around the photographs.

Using computers and electronic archives

Computer technology (eg HyperCard) now allows us to produce 'talking books' complete with computer graphics, where the computer will 'speak' out loud in the voice of the person who recorded the story. This is a very useful additional aid for language learning. It would be possible to create a 'talking dictionary'.

The Kaurna vocabulary, and that of many other Aboriginal and Torres Strait Islander languages, has already been loaded into an electronic archive. There is a good chance that you can obtain the vocabulary of your language on a computer disk. This allows you to search and find particular words or endings of words. If you learn how to manipulate the files, you can sort them into different categories to suit your purposes (eg pull out all the fish terms).

Language nests — Kohunga reo

Maori language revival started in the 1970s. The backbone of the Maori language revival is the Kohunga reo 'language nests' which began in 1982. They link the grandparent generation with the preschoolers, so that the very young learn from the most knowledgeable older generation. Kohunga reo have produced a new generation of Maori speakers who know more Maori than their parents' generation. Around 1982, a bare handful of children came to primary school with any knowledge of Maori. In 1989, 2000–3000 children, many of them fluent bilinguals, were starting school after having been exposed to daily use of the Maori language for three years or more (Spolsky 1989: 91).

Kohunga reo have been very successful in producing fluent bilingual children. This puts pressure on local schools to establish a bilingual language program. They seek to both re-establish the number of speakers (through teaching in school) and to increase the number of public and official functions for which Maori is used.

To what degree you can copy the Maori experience depends on how many fluent speakers remain and how much of the language survives in the community. If a language is to become re-established, it means changing patterns of language use. This will be very difficult at first. The revival of Hebrew as an everyday spoken language began with one man,

Ben Yehuda, around the turn of the century. He made a conscious decision to use Hebrew and insisted from that point on that Hebrew was spoken by his own family. He made a point of using it in public whether other people understood it or not. In fact, he and his family went out of their way to speak Hebrew, and their efforts had a major formative influence in the development of the modern Israeli language. Of course, the situation in Israel is very different to Aboriginal Australia, but there are important lessons here. Remember, the important thing is to use your language whenever and wherever you can.

For more ideas have a look at materials developed in specific languages (eg Djabugay). Also, a draft kit, *Let's Talk Our Language*, developed by Kathryn Gale and Beth Graham, contains a lot of good ideas suitable for a range of different language situations. The Western Australian *Framework for the Teaching of Aboriginal Languages in Primary Schools* also details a range of games, activities and teaching strategies. ■

Tabaretti Yaitya Warra Wodli — Snooky Varcoeityarnungko

26 February 1993

Yella ngaiinni nguinya mankondi.

> Today it gives me great pleasure.

Marni na purrutye budni tabaretti Yaitya Warra Wodliko.

> I'd like to welcome you all to the opening of the South Australian
> Aboriginal Language Centre.

Marni yerlteriburka South Australiako Lyn Arnold budni.

> I'd like to welcome the Premier of South Australia, Lyn Arnold.

Marni yerlteriburka Aboriginal Affairsko Kym Mayes budni.

> I'd like to welcome the Minister of Aboriginal Affairs, Kym Mayes.

Marni pangkarra Yerltabultiburka Rod Sawford budni.

> I'd like to welcome the member for Port Adelaide, Rod Sawford.

Wiwurra manko mankorendi ia yellara. Tauere marni.

> A great many people have gathered together for this event today.
> That's really good.

Gadla Kaurna meyunna Mikawommangga paininggianna yakko ngadlendi. Warlto ngadluko muinmonendi medarnendi. Ngadlu wingko palta paltarendi ngadluko warra. Ngadlu tadlanyanna padlondi warra wanggandi. Ngadlu yurrenna padlondi warra yurringgarendi. Ngadlu muka mukanna wingko tikkandi muka Kaurnarli. Ngadlu padlondi mukabandi warra Kaurnako.

> The campfires of the Kaurna people on the plains around Port
> Adelaide have long since gone out, but we can still feel the warmth
> in our hearts. We long for our languages again. Our tongues long to
> say the words. Our ears want to hear the words. Our brains still
> think as Kaurna brains. We want to remember the Kaurna language.

Ngadlu kundo punggorendi. Ngadlu tudno bidnandi iako. Ngadluko tangkuinya tanendi.

> Our hearts are heavy. We have long been waiting for this occasion.
> Our dreams are becoming reality. ■

Nicholas Thieberger

Using computers

Using computers

nce you have found sources of information on the language you are interested in, you will want to do something with the information.

You may want to produce a book of stories, or a dictionary, or combine tapes with written material to help teach the language.

You should use a computer to help with all of these jobs. For more information about using computers with Australian languages, see 'Notes for the Computer-assisted Language Worker' (Thieberger 1994b). It goes into more detail than we can here.

Any computer will have a word-processing programme which allows you to type information, and then rearrange it and print it out neatly. Some word-processing programmes are easier to use than others; some let you do page layout, including drawings or photographs.

If you are producing a wordlist you can use a database programme, which will sort and locate information very quickly. Databases are very useful for entering wordlists or dictionaries, as they provide a form on the screen for the information to fit in. Relational databases allow you to link different types of information, or to use a single English list and link it to lists of other languages. This could be useful for areas where there are many sources, or where there could be a number of dialects.

For wordlists you can also use a text file in which entries are marked as belonging to certain fields (a method called field-oriented standard format or FOSF). Many wordlists and dictionaries of Australian languages are done in this way. It has the advantage of allowing the work to be done on any computer, with any word-processing software (see below for an example).

When you are typing up your texts, dictionary or wordlist, try to include as much information as possible. Each word in the list should have a source (either a text number, or a person), and other useful additional information. Remember that it is much easier to take information out than it is to put it in when you have 2000 entries in your dictionary.

For printing you should use a laser printer, and for publications you may even need to send the work to a bureau to make high-resolution bromides, as laser printing can be too fuzzy for high-quality reproduction.

If you want to link sound to texts (speaking linked to written versions of the speech) then you can use 'multimedia' or 'interactive' software. On Macintosh computers, HyperCard is a programme which allows you to link pictures, video clips, sounds and texts. Examples of the type of links you can make between story texts and sound are *Australia's Languages: Australian Indigenous Languages Information Stacks* (on floppy disks) and also the *Encyclopaedia of Aboriginal Australia* (on CD), both produced by AIATSIS.

You should always think of your computer files as resources which must be kept safely. Backup your work onto at least one other copy. Make safe copies of important work and store them in a different place to your computer. If your language centre or office burns down, what will you have left!

You can deposit copies of your work at AIATSIS. They offer a free service of safe deposit for electronic data in their electronic data archive (ASEDA).

Case study

n this section we will look at an example of how to change a handwritten manuscript into a computer-based text file.

The manuscript was found in the Benedictine monastery at New Norcia in Western Australia by Bob Dixon. There are five parts to the manuscript — two are alphabetical by language to Italian, and two are Italian to language, however each contains different amounts of information, with substantial overlap between them. The fifth is an entirely different language, which looks like one of the Nyungar languages of the south-west; it is not dealt with further here. I visited New Norcia to get a better copy of the manuscript and to discuss the access restrictions and copyright issues.

There are no clues on the cover of the work to indicate who wrote it or when. The one clue about when it was written is the reference to 'Pintangadenga: the name of the station owned by Mr Padbury'. Brown and Geytenbeek (1990) list Pinyjangartangkanya as the place where the De Grey house was built. Padbury owned a station on the De Grey River (within Ngarla territory), between 1863 and 1868. Hence we can tentatively date the manuscript as late 1860s.

The New Norcia manuscript.

The vocabulary is given with Italian equivalents, and the Aboriginal language is written using an Italian-based spelling system. We can see that words that we know today, like *jina* for 'foot', are reflected by *cina* in this list. Fortunately, Italian spelling is much more suited to recording Aboriginal languages for most sounds, so that we can accurately predict most of the correspondences between the wordlist and what sounds are meant to be represented. The problem of retroflex sounds remains, as there appears to be no recognition of them by the writer. Some double *r* sounds have an overbar ($\bar{rr}$), but the combination of both wordlists shows that the same word may have an overbar in one version but not in the other.

On the previous page you can see an image of a page of the manuscript. The two lists of language to Italian were read, translated and typed, then keyboarded using tabs to separate the three fields of language, Italian and English (a database is a good way to enter information like this, with a separate field for each of the fields of language). They were proofread twice from this keyboarded version back to the original. Any illegible items were marked. Because there are four versions of the same wordlist, it was possible to cross-check spellings and illegible characters. Proofreading is very important, and it is usually better to have one person type a work and another person proofread it.

Using the structure of the manuscript, each word or phrase (Ngarla word, Italian word, English word) was marked with codes

(\w for headword, \i for Italian, \g for English). This set up the file in categories which we will call fields.

The two files were combined, and an additional field added by duplicating the \w or language field. This new field was used for reworking the spelling into one that is closer to the one in use in the Pilbara today, as much as is possible. Note that the original headword was kept in the file. Structuring the text in this way means that we can work with it as we would with a database. In addition, we can manipulate information within the fields using a word processor like Nisus which lets us search for text with a regular shape even if the content varies. A regular expression like this:

$$\backslash z [^\backslash\backslash]*cci[^\backslash\backslash]*$$

locates the text *cci* within the newly added(\z) field, and allows changes to be made only to that string.

Ordinarily we would think of *gn* at the beginning of a word reflecting what we write today as *ng*, but in Italian, *gn* is the sound of *ni* in onion. So we would write the word *gniupa* as *nyupa*, the current word for 'spouse' in parts of the Pilbara.

Global changes made to the \z field are: *chi* became *ki*; *ci* became *ji* (not when preceded by *c* and when followed by a consonant); *ci* followed by a vowel became *j* (not when preceded by *c*); *gl* and *gli* became *ly*; *gn* became *ny*; *j* became *y*; *o* became *u*. Vowel combinations were separated by a glide (*ia* became *iya*) and glides were inserted before vowel intial words.

Duplicate entries were deleted using the regular expression function of Nisus. The whole file was reversed to alphabetise on the English field, permitting duplicate entries to be deleted or collapsed. Definitions of verbs were changed to allow alphabetising on the main word rather than on 'to'. No other effort was put into the reversal, but a preferable finderlist would elaborate on the existing one by breaking up senses into greater detail.

A list of 166 words was taken from this combined file and used to compare with other languages of the Pilbara. One hundred and sixty-six words of a number of regional languages were placed into a spreadsheet file (following the procedure adopted by Menning and Nash in the IAD Central Australian sourcebook). Of the 166 words, 17 could not be found in the manuscript. The following table shows the number of correspondences between the manuscript list and the other language lists; the first figure is the number of correspondences, the second is the number of unique correspondences (the number of times that language was the only one to reflect the language of the manuscript):

Banyjima	40/1
Manyjilyjarra	24/0
Martuthunira	10/0
Ngarla	85/42
Ngarluma	41/6
Nyangumarta	27/2
Warnman	25/1
Yindjibarndi	24/0

It is clear that the highest correspondence is with Ngarla (as represented in Brown and Geytenbeek's 1990 Ngarla–English dictionary), but there are still 60/166 words which are not reflected in the Ngarla list. These figures also show that Ngarla was the only language to correspond with words of the manuscript in 42 cases.

The differences between the old manuscript and modern Ngarla could be a result of:

- language change over the 120 years between collection of information;
- several dialects of Ngarla may have existed, of which only one survives today;
- the definitions in the old manuscript and the current dictionary of Ngarla may be sufficiently different to prevent comparisons.

Whatever is the case, the fact that the wordlist is legible and in electronic form, means that it will be easier for others to work with it from now on.

The vocabulary is available in electronic form as a backslash marked-up file from the Aboriginal Studies Electronic Data Archive. Depositing with ASEDA means that others can have access to the work and can reproduce it in different forms.

Technical details

A tab-separated file in a form like **(a)** can be manipulated using a regular expression parser like Nisus or Qued/M, both types of software that run on Macintosh computers. The structured set of information **(a)** becomes the marked up data set **(b)** using the following regular expression:

find: ^\(.:+\)\t\(.:+\)\t\(.:+\)\\r,

replace with: \\w \l \t\\l \2\t\\i \3\r

(a)	mirror	c'alachi o c'alai	specchio
	miser	c'umar`e	avaro, tenace
	moon	w'ill`or`o, w'il`orr	luna
	morass	gnitura	morass

(b)	\w mirror	\l c'alachi o c'alai	\i specchio
	\w miser	\l c'umar`e	\i avaro, tenace
	\w moon	\l w'ill`or`o, w'il`orr	\i luna
	\w morass	\l gnitura	\i morass

You can then decide to make the headwords bold or italic, to underline the definitions or whatever. The important thing to remember is that you are creating a file of data, not just the finished product that you want printed out on a page. If you make sure that you have a good data file, then you can create lists of words in the language, with definitions, or you can create lists of words in English, with their language meanings (a finderlist). See Notes for the Computer-assisted Language Worker (Thieberger 1994b) for more information about text manipulation and working with dictionaries and wordlists. ∎

Appendices

Appendix I
List of participants AIATSIS Paper & Talk Workshop 3–5 March 1993

Amery, Rob	Australian Languages Framework, SSABSA, Adelaide
Austin, Peter	Linguistics Department, La Trobe University, Melbourne
Bancroft, Robyne	AIATSIS
Brady, Pat	AIATSIS
Brown, Michelle	Tasmanian Aboriginal Centre
Calgaret, Tony	Nyungar Language and Cultural Centre, Bunbury, WA
Cann, Julie	Tasmanian Aboriginal Centre
Cope, Wendy	Aboriginal Adult Education, Tasmania
Cozier, Harold	Wellington, NSW
Couzens, Ivan	Warnambool, Vic
Crowley, Terry	Linguistics Department, University of Waikato
Dargin, Lawrie	AIATSIS
Donaldson, Tamsin	AIATSIS
Donovan, Frances	Wauchope, NSW
Donovan, Robert	Wauchope NSW
Duroux, Mary	Moruya, NSW
Gray, Tony	Wauchope, NSW
Harris, Alana	AIATSIS
Highfold, Robert	Native Title, Land Heritage and Environment, ATSIC
Hosking, Dianne	AIATSIS
Humes, Bill	AIATSIS
Ingram, Sharon	AIATSIS
Jonas, Bill	AIATSIS
Mansell, Brett	Tasmanian Aboriginal Centre
McIver, Glenys	AIATSIS
McKeown, Frank	AIATSIS
O'Connor, Patricia	Rochedale, Brisbane

Raymond, Lorna	AIATSIS
Reid, Bill	Bourke, NSW
Sculthorpe, June	Tasmanian Aboriginal Centre
Simpson, Jane	Linguistics Department, Sydney University
Smith, Sandra	Victorian Museum
Thearle, Rhonda	Wellington, NSW
Thieberger, Nicholas	AIATSIS
Triffitt, Geraldine	AIATSIS
Troman, Edmund	Tasmanian Aboriginal Centre
Troy, Jaki	Native Title, Land Heritage and Environment, ATSIC
Walker, Emily	Sherwood, NSW
Walker, Ken	Bowraville, NSW
Walker, Michael	Tabulam, NSW
Williams, Cheryl	AIATSIS

List of participants AIATSIS Paper & Talk Workshop 3–5 March 1993

Appendix 2
Examples of published and unpublished work based on reworked historical sources

This is not a comprehensive list, but it is meant to provide examples of work of the kind discussed in this book. Many of the following are available in electronic form from ASEDA at AIATSIS.

Austin, P 1993, *A Dictionary of Gamilaraay, Northern New South Wales.* Bundoora: Department of Linguistics, La Trobe University.

Austin, P 1993, *A Reference Dictionary of Gamilaraay, Northern New South Wales.* Bundoora: Department of Linguistics, La Trobe University.

Bell, J 1994, *A Dictionary of the Gubbi Gubbi and Butchulla Languages.* Brisbane: J Bell.

Bindon, P and R Chadwick 1992, *A Nyoongar Wordlist from the South-west of Western Australia [Nyoongar/English].* Perth: Anthropology Department, Western Australian Museum.

Bishop, I 1990, Koongurrukun Language — Lexicon Letters K through to Y. Canberra: copy held in AIATSIS library.

Blake, BJ 1991, Woiwurrung, the Melbourne Language. In RMW Dixon and Barry J Blake (eds), *The Handbook of Australian Languages,* vol 4. Melbourne: Oxford University Press. 30–122.

Blake, BJ 1979. Pitta-Pitta. In RMW Dixon and Barry J Blake (eds), *The Handbook of Australian Languages,* vol 1. Canberra: Australian National University Press. 183–242.

Brasch SL 1991, Working Papers from Thesis on Gureng Gureng: Vocabularies South-east Queensland Languages and Working Papers: Vocabulary Bunganditj, South Australia

[Gureng Gureng/Bunganditj//English]. Canberra: copy held in AIATSIS library.

Dench, A 1994, Nyungar. In *Macquarie Aboriginal Words: A Dictionary of Words of Aboriginal and Torres Strait Islander Languages.* Sydney: Macquarie Library.

Eades, D 1976, *The Dharawal and Dhurga Languages of the New South Wales South Coast*. Canberra: AIAS.

Fitzpatrick, P 1989, *Warra Kaurna: A Selected Wordlist from the Language of the Kaurna People of the Adelaide Plains [Kaurna/English]*. Adelaide: Department of Environment and Planning.

Gell, JP 1988, The Vocabulary of the Adelaide Tribe, *Journal of the Anthropological Society of South Australia* 25(5), 3–15.

Hall, HA and CG von Brandenstein, 1971, *A Partial Vocabulary of the Ngalooma Aboriginal Tribe*. Canberra: AIAS.

Hercus, LA 1992, *A Nukunu Dictionary*. Canberra: L Hercus.

Hercus, LA 1992, *Wembawemba Dictionary*. Canberra: L Hercus.

Hercus, LA 1993, *Paakantyi Dictionary*. Canberra: L Hercus.

Hercus, LA Wergaia Vocabulary 1. Work in progress.

Hercus, LA (nd), Southern Ngarigu Vocabulary. Canberra: copy held in AIATSIS library.

Hercus, LA (nd), Yarluyandi Vocabulary. Canberra: copy held in AIATSIS library.

Hosking, D and S McNicol 1993, *Wiradjuri*. Canberra: D Hosking and S McNicol.

Johnson, S and A Lissarrague (nd), Yaygir Vocabulary. Canberra: copy held in AIATSIS library.

Kohen, JL 1993, *A Dictionary of the Dharug Language: The Inland Dialect*. Winmalee: Three Sisters Productions. 147–60.

Kohen, JL 1993, *A Dictionary of the Gundungurra Language*. Winmalee: Three Sisters Productions. 136–46.

Lissarrague, A 1994, A Dhanggadi Dictionary. Canberra: copy held in AIATSIS library.

Meier, A 1977, Vocabulary of the Dieri Tribe. Canberra: copy held in AIATSIS library.

Moorhouse, M and J Simpson, Ngaiawang vocabulary. Work in progress.

Nekes, H, EA Worms, L de Veer and W McGrego (nd), Vocabularies of Nyul Nyul and other Kimberley Languages, from Nekes and Worms, and J Bischofs manuscripts. Work in progress.

Plomley, NJB 1976, *A Word-list of the Tasmanian Aboriginal Languages*. Hobart: Self published.

Reuther, JG, PA Scherer (tr), L Hercus and P Austin (nd),The Diari. Work in progress.

Schürmann, C, J Simpson and G O'Grady (nd), A Vocabulary of the Parnkalla Language. Work in progress.

Simpson, J and R Amery 1994, Kaurna. In *Macquarie Aboriginal Words: A Dictionary of Words of Aboriginal and Torres Strait Islander Languages*. Sydney: Macquarie Library.

Simpson, J, JM Black and GN O'Grady (nd), Wirrung Wordlist. Work
    in progress.

Teichelmann, C, C Schürmann and J Simpson (nd), Kaurna
    vocabulary. Work in progress.

Troy, J 1994, The Sydney Language. In *Macquarie Aboriginal Words: A
    Dictionary of Words of Aboriginal and Torres Strait Islander
    Languages*. Sydney: Macquarie Library.

Appendix 3
Sources and
contacts

ere are some sources that will be useful in your search for material on your language:

Blake, BJ 1991, *Australian Aboriginal Languages: A General Introduction*, second edition. Brisbane: University Queensland Press.

Dixon, RMW 1980, *The Languages of Australia*. Cambridge: Cambridge University Press.

Yallop C 1981, *Australian Aboriginal Languages*. London: Andre Deutsch.

ere are contacts for organisations that will be useful in your search for material on your language (this list was produced by the Yamaji Language Centre):

New South Wales

Niigarr Lingo Gumbi
    NSW Aboriginal Language Management Committee
    84 Derribong Street, Trangie NSW 2823
    Phone: (068) 887 136

Muurbay Aboriginal Language and Culture Co-op, Ltd.
    648 Sherwood Road, Sherwood via Kempsey NSW 2440
    Phone: (065) 669 353   Fax: (065) 669 143

Northern Territory

Darwin Regional Aboriginal Language Association
    Phone: (089) 814 142   Fax: (089) 817 031

East Arnhem Language Centre

    via Yirrkala School, PO Box 936, Nhulunbuy NT 0881

    Phone: (089) 871 224   Fax: (089) 871 725

Institute for Aboriginal Development

    PO Box 2531, Alice Springs NT 0871

    Phone: (089) 522 688   Fax: (089) 531 884

Kardu Numida Incorporated

    OLSH c/o the Brothers, Port Keats NT 0822

    Phone: (089) 782 477; 782 363   Fax: (089) 782 300

Katherine Regional Aboriginal Language Centre

    PO Box 89, Katherine NT 0851

    Phone: (089) 711 233   Fax: (089) 710 561

Nauiyu Nanbiya Language Centre

    PMB 28, Daly River NT 0822

    Phone: (089) 782 427   Fax: (089) 782 590

Papulu Apparr-Kari Language Centre

    c/o PO Box 1108, Tennant Creek NT 0861

    Phone: (089) 623 270   Fax: (089) 623 280

West Arnhem

    Minjilang, Croker Island via Darwin NT 0822

    Phone: (089) 790 299; 790 295   Fax: (089) 790 297

    Contact: Mary Yarmirr

Queensland

Djabugay Tribal Aboriginal Co-op

    PO Box 34, Kuranda Qld 4872

    Phone: (070) 938 806; 938 859   Fax: (070) 937 629

Guugu Yimidhirr Language Centre

c/o PO Hopevale, Qld 4871

Phone: (070) 609 261; 609 232   Fax: (070) 609 262

Kombumerri Aboriginal Corporation for Culture

154 Rochedale Road, Rochedale Qld 4123

Phone: (07) 341 5575   Fax: (07) 341 9385

Thoorgine Education Centre

PO Box 363, Pialba Qld 4655

Phone: (071) 244 100   Fax: (071) 244 100

Torres Strait Islander Art & Craft Corporation

PO Box 5647, MC Townsville Qld 4810

Phone: (077) 786 68   Fax: (077) 814 033

South Australia

Yaitya Warra Wodli

1 Lipson Street, Port Adelaide SA 5015

Phone: (08) 241 0227   Fax: (08) 241 0228

Tasmania

Tasmanian Aboriginal Language Program, Head Office

198 Elizabeth Street or GPO Box 569F, Hobart Tas 7001

Phone: (002) 348 311   Fax: (002) 311 348

Contact: June Sculthorpe (Program Co-ordinator);

Sally Clarke

North & North-West Region

163 John Street or PO Box 531, Launceston Tas 7250

Phone: (003) 316 966   Fax: (003) 314 258

Victoria

Lordjba Victoria

    PO Box 15, Healesville Vic 3777

    Phone: (03) 646 7255; mobile: (018) 580 893

    Fax: (03) 646 7266

Western Australia

Fitzroy Crossing Annexe of KLRC

    PO Box 86, Fitzroy Crossing WA 6765

    Phone: (091) 915 124

    E-mail: klrchc@peg.pegasus.oz.au

Kimberley Language Resource Centre

    PMB 11, Hall's Creek WA 6770

    Phone: (091) 686 005   Fax: (091) 686 023

    E-mail: klrchc@peg.pegasus.oz.au

Mirima Dawang Woorlab-gerring

    PO Box 162, Kununurra WA 6743

    Phone: (091) 691 029   Fax: (091) 682 639

    E-mail: mdwg@peg.pegasus.oz.au

Noongar Language & Culture Centre

    16 Little Street, Carey Park, Bunbury WA 6230

    Phone: (097) 912 165

Wangka Maya Pilbara Aboriginal Language Centre

    PO Box 693, Port Hedland WA 6721

    Phone: (091) 732 621   Fax: (091) 732 973

    E-mail: alcphang@peg.pegasus.oz.au

Wangkanyi Ngurra Tjurta Aboriginal Corporation
PMB 3, Kalgoorlie WA 6430
Phone: (090) 211 655   Fax: (090) 218 128

Yamaji Language Centre
PO Box 433, Geraldton WA 6530
Phone: (099) 643 550, 214 477   Fax: (099) 642 634
E-mail: yamaji@peg.pegasus.oz.au

Amery, R 1986, Languages in Contact — the Case of Kintore and Papunya. In *Language in Aboriginal Australia* 1, 13–38.

Austin, P 1992, *A Dictionary of Yinggarda*. Bundoora: Department of Linguistics, La Trobe University.

Black, P 1983, *Aboriginal Languages of the Northern Territory*. SAL: Batchelor.

Brown, A and B Geytenbeek 1990, Ngarla/English Dictionary, interim edition. Port Hedland: Wangka Maya, Pilbara Aboriginal Language Centre.

Capell, A 1963, *Linguistic Survey of Australia*. Canberra: AIAS.

Crowley, T 1992, *An Introduction to Historical Linguistics*. Auckland: Oxford University Press.

Edwards, R 1971, The hero Tjilbruke, *Origin* 4(6), 13.

Gale, K and B Graham (nd), Lets Talk Our Language: Language Survival Strategies for Aboriginal Languages, Draft kit.

Gerritsen, R 1994, *And Their Ghosts May Be Heard*. Fremantle: Fremantle Arts Centre Press.

Jones, E 1989, *The Story of the Falling Star*. Canberra: Aboriginal Studies Press.

McGregor, W 1988, *Handbook of Kimberley Languages*, Pacific Linguistics C-105. Canberra: Pacific Linguistics.

Menning, K and D Nash 1981, *Sourcebook for Central Australian Languages*. Alice Springs: IAD.

References

Ngarrindjeri, Narrunga and Kaurna Languages Project 1990, *Narrunga, Kaurna & Ngarrindjeri Songs*. Elizabeth, SA: Ngarrindjeri, Narrunga and Kaurna Languages Project.

O'Grady, G 1960, New Concepts in Nyangumada, *Anthropological Linguistics* 2, 1–6

O'Grady, GN, CF Voegelin and FM Voegelin 1966, Languages of the World: Indo-Pacific fascicle 6, *Anthropological Linguistics*, 8(2), 1–197.

Oates, LF 1975, *The 1973 Supplement to a Revised Linguistic Survey of Australia*. Armidale: Christian Book Centre.

Rowley, T 1992, *An Introduction to Historical Linguistics*. Oxford: Oxford University Press.

Schürmann, CW 1844, *A Vocabulary of the Parnkalla Language, Spoken by the Natives Inhabiting the Western Shores of Spencer's Gulf. To which is Prefixed a Collection of Grammatical Rules, Hitherto Ascertained*. Adelaide: George Dehane.

Simpson, J 1985, How Warumungu People Express New Concepts, *Language in Central Australia* 4, 12–25.

Smith, D and B Halstead 1990, *Lookin for Your Mob*. Canberra: AIATSIS.

Spolsky, B 1989, Maori Bilingual Education and Language Revitalisation, *Journal of Multilingual and Multicultural Development* 10(2), 89–106

Teichelmann, CG, and CW Schürmann 1840, *Outlines of a Grammar, Vocabulary, and Phraseology, of the Aboriginal Language of South Australia, Spoken by the Natives in and for Some Distance Around Adelaide*. Adelaide: Published by the authors, at the native location.

Thieberger, N 1993, *Handbook of WA Aboriginal Languages South of the Kimberley Region*, Pacific Linguistics C-124. Canberra: Pacific Linguistics.

Thieberger, N 1994a, *Australia's Languages: Australian Indigenous Languages Information Stacks*, (HyperCard interactive multimedia). Canberra: AIATSIS.

Thieberger, N 1994b, Notes for the Computer-assisted Language Worker, ms.

Tindale, NB 1974, *Aboriginal Tribes of Australia*. Canberra: ANU Press.

Troy, J 1994, *The Sydney Language*. Canberra: J Troy.

Western Australia. Ministry of Education and Australia. Department of Employment, Education and Training 1992, *Framework for the Teaching of Aboriginal Languages in Primary Schools*. East Perth: Ministry of Education, Western Australia.

Wurm, SA 1972, *Languages of Australia and Tasmania*. The Hague: Mouton.

Wyatt, W 1879, *Vocabulary of the Adelaide and Encounter Bay Tribes, with a Few Words of that of Rapid Bay*. In JD Woods (ed), *The Native Tribes of South Australia*. Adelaide: 169–182.

Yallop, C 1993, The Structure of Australian Aboriginal Languages. In M Walsh and C Yallop (eds), *Language and Culture in Aboriginal Australia*. Canberra: Aboriginal Studies Press.

www.ingramcontent.com/pod-product-compliance
Lightning Source LLC
Chambersburg PA
CBHW052033280526
45791CB00010B/2953